Not Too Long Ago

Not Too Long Ago

STORIES OF A TRADITIONAL WAY OF LIFE

GARRY CRANFORD

FLANKER PRESS LIMITED
ST. JOHN'S

Library and Archives Canada Cataloguing in Publication

Not too long ago [electronic resource] : stories of a traditional way of
life / Garry Cranford, [editor]. -- 2nd ed.

Includes index.
Includes Our lives (originally published 2000).
Electronic monograph.
Issued also in print format.
ISBN 978-1-926881-99-7 (PDF).--ISBN 978-1-926881-69-0 (EPUB).--
ISBN 978-1-926881-70-6 (MOBI)
1. Newfoundland and Labrador--Social life and customs--Anecdotes.
2. Newfoundland and Labrador--History--Anecdotes. I. Cranford, Garry,
1950- . II. Title: Our lives.

FC2168.N68 2012   971.8   C2012-901122-3

© 2012 by Garry Cranford

PRINTED IN CANADA

Illustrated by Bob Pope
Cover Design: Peter Hanes

FLANKER PRESS LTD.
PO BOX 2522, STATION C
ST. JOHN'S, NL
CANADA

WWW.FLANKERPRESS.COM

First Edition printed in 1999.

4 5 6 7 8 9 10 11

Canada   Canada Council   Conseil des Arts   Newfoundland
             for the Arts   du Canada   Labrador

The publisher acknowledges the financial support of the Government of Canada through the Canada
Book Fund (CBF) and the Government of Newfoundland and Labrador, Department of Tourism, Culture, Industry and Innovation for our publishing activities. We acknowledge the support of the Canada
Council for the Arts, which last year invested $157 million to bring the arts to Canadians throughout the
country. Nous remercions le Conseil des arts du Canada de son soutien. L'an dernier, le Conseil a investi
157 millions de dollars pour mettre de l'art dans la vie des Canadiennes et des Canadiens de tout le pays.

PREFACE

In 1998, I was engaged by the Seniors Resource Centre, based in St. John's, Newfoundland and Labrador, to interview and record recollections of seniors around the province, especially those involved in some way with the association's outreach program. To facilitate this, the Seniors Resource Centre put out a call through its outreach programs for volunteers, and asked outreach leaders to refer me to persons in their communities who might not otherwise come forward.

I spent that year travelling around the province, visiting seniors in their homes, and taping interviews. I was briefed on the backgrounds of these seniors and the highlights of their experiences. In Bonavista, I interviewed fishermen; in Burin, seniors with memories of the 1929 tsunami; in Labrador, stories of the trapline; on the west coast, stories of experiences in World War II; and in Twillingate, a lighthouse keeper. These people shared their stories of a pioneering way of life, raising families in hard times, stories of close calls while engaging in sealing, and, of course, wherever I went, I asked for ghost stories.

The purpose of the Seniors Resource Centre project was to collect stories of high interest from seniors with which other seniors would identify, and therefore encourage them to become engaged in reading. Another outcome was to produce a lasting social studies collection of interest to future readers, students, and researchers of Newfoundland and Labrador culture.

The end result was over 100 hours of taped interviews, and hundreds of pages of transcribed conversations. From there I edited the transcribed texts, and a panel of seniors selected those they found most interesting. Setting priorities, a collection of stories found its way into book form, titled *Not Too Long Ago*, and its length was determined by the budget available for a book.

Because there was so much additional incredible material left unpublished, Flanker Press took it upon itself to produce a supplementary book titled *Our Lives*, featuring stories that had been culled and excluded from the initial selection.

Both books are now combined in this new, expanded and revised edition. Royalties from the sale of this book will go to support programs of the Seniors Resource Centre.

GARRY CRANFORD
FEBRUARY, 2012

ACKNOWLEDGEMENTS

I wish to thank the 66 seniors who contributed to *Not Too Long Ago*. It is said that experience is a great teacher. If so, your experiences are about to give readers a great education in Newfoundland and Labrador history and culture.

All of you have greeted me in your homes, and offered an open invitation to return. I would like to thank you for your hospitality.

On behalf of generations to come, I congratulate you on your contributions to this book.

Producing *Not Too Long Ago* took the co-operation of many people across the province. This would not have been possible without those who know our communities and who know our seniors. I wish to thank Joan McLean of Northwest River and Janet Skinner and Donna Paddon of Happy Valley–Goose Bay. In Cartwright, Jessie Bird also recommended many wonderful people to be interviewed.

Across Newfoundland, contributors were recommended by our network of seniors, peer advocates, community leaders, and personal contacts: Barbara Barrett, Arnold's Cove; Linda Bath, Bonavista; Dorothy Bonnell, Bell Island; Peggy Doucette, Port au Port; Theresa Greeley, Gander; Evelyn Grondin-Bailey, Burin; Harriett Greene, Port aux Basques; Stella Hollett, Burin; Catherine Pennell, Trepassey; Philip Power, Grand Falls; Gladys Snow, Rocky Harbour; and Jim Young of Twillingate. Thank you all.

I would like to thank Coordinator Doris Hapgood, the teachers, and the students of the Rabbittown Learners Programme who workshopped the material. Thanks to Pam Rideout and Janet Goosney of Teachers On Wheels, and Suzanne Sexty and the other members of the Seniors Resource Centre Literacy Committee. Thanks to our readers: Hazel Blackwood, Evelyn Percy, Rick Simon, Brigitta Schmid, and Mary Woodruff. Don McDonald and David White of the Literacy Development Council also offered valuable feedback and comments. I also appreciate the technical advice from Dr. Philip Hiscock of the Department of Folklore, Memorial University. For her overall encouragement and direction, thanks to Rosemary Lester, Executive Director of the Seniors Resource Centre. Thanks to volunteer Jerry Cranford for the design and layout of the book, and to Margo Cranford and Vera McDonald for reading final drafts.

Financial support for this project has been provided by the National Literacy Secretariat (Human Resources Development Canada) and the Literacy Development Council of Newfoundland and Labrador.

THE STORIES AND THEIR ORGANIZATION

The stories in *Not Too Long Ago* were collected from seniors across the province, primarily through taped interviews, supplemented by written submissions. The reading style is as varied as the storyteller, and edited as little as possible, in an effort to retain the original flavour of the conversation. In all, there are 66 contributions.

In addition to those contributors for the literacy project, I have included an interview I conducted with my grandmother, Mildred Cranford, who talks about "In Service" and "On the Labrador."

The goal of this project was to bring together, under one cover, a collection of stories that represented a culture to which mature Newfoundland and Labrador readers could easily relate. By doing so, it is hoped that the content will have as high an interest level as possible to those readers this book is aimed at: the adult reader.

All major regions of the province are represented. In the original editon of *Not Too Long Ago*, the stories were grouped into geographic regions, but in this editon, the stories are arranged alphabetically by contributor, and generally, are much expanded, by bringing together those stories from the second collection, *Our Lives*.

For ease of identifying the geographic location of the stories, or where the contributors lived when they were interviewed, we have included an index, and to further enhance the indexing, we have greatly expanded the table of contents to show topics discussed, which usually easily identifies where the stories come from.

CONTENTS

KATHLEEN ABBOTT

RETIRED?

Kathleen Abbott of Port au Port West is a very active senior. She is the driving force behind the restoration of Our Lady of Mercy Museum. She has big plans for the convent and Our Lady of Mercy Church. But she wasn't always interested. I visited Kathleen at the museum.

I WASN'T ALL THAT interested at first. I started working on the museum project the year I retired from teaching, 1990. This museum used to be the rectory. It had been rented out several times and it was ready to be demolished.

I was called for a meeting and I said yes. I was voted in as chairperson and I've been here ever since. It was quite a challenge, and gets to be more of a challenge every year. I always had something to do, because I had four children and I had to raise them as a single parent. My husband died over 45 years ago.

THE OUR LADY OF MERCY MUSEUM

FIRST OF ALL, WE STARTED on the museum. The sun porch was falling down. Right away we had to look for project funding and there wasn't a lot of money.

We started sending out feelers through the church bulletin. We asked people to bring in information and pictures. And we got what we could from the schools.

Right now our high school is closing and we have made a deal with the principal that the trophies and the pictures will come here. There is always something coming in so we can freshen the displays, or develop new ones. Parishioners are taking a lot of pride in it now, especially since it has become a provincial heritage structure.

Each year we do something different to encourage visitors. We have a tea room which we will open next week. We serve tea in pots and we serve old-fashioned recipes.

SHOWER OF ROSES

THERE WAS A LOT OF DEVOTION to St. Theresa with our traditional priests back in the late 1800s. She is one of our youngest saints because she died when she was 24. In 1997, she was made a Doctor of the Church, and that is really something.

Doing the grotto was one of my goals, but it was really begun by Father Joy, because of a miracle that happened to him.

Father was kneeling, giving his thanksgiving one morning after mass, and he was sick at the time. He was praying, and all of a sudden he had a vision. In the vision, he got a perfume smell of roses and a shower of rose petals fell at his feet. When he described it to the parishioners the next Sunday, he told them he didn't know what the reason was.

He said it was either that St. Theresa wanted the people to pray more, or that she wanted something erected in her honour. Right away he took up a collection and he got $1,000 and put up a statue. The St. Theresa's statue in the church came from Rome. Devotions to St. Theresa continue to this day.

In my mind, if Father Joy thought it was important, we should also have something outside the church. So, we built a grotto to St. Theresa in front of the museum.

INGE BARTH

Many Newfoundlanders and Labradorians had hard lives. Mrs. Inge Barth had a hard life, but it was different from that of most people. She sent along a story of her life for other seniors to read. Here is a part of what she wrote about her life, and starting out in Labrador.

I WAS BORN IN Germany in 1928. My father was called Fritz Schreiber and my mother was called Mimi. We had three farms: an animal farm, an agricultural farm, and a farm to grow food for the animals.

Life was wonderful! I began to train St. Bernard dogs. There was much work, and I earned very much money. My day began at 5:00 when I got up. At the first farm I trained horses for the German Army. Then my father died and I was in charge of three big farms, a herd of sheep, and I had 400 workers. They treated me very well. At first I was afraid they would not take my orders, because I was only 15 years old.

This all happened during the Second World War. We provided food for the German Army. It was a very bad time. At the same time, the Russians invaded Eastern Germany and they took all the animals. I was captured and they sent me to the camps in Russia.

I worked in the mines for about 12 hours every day of the week. This happened in Siberia, to the north of Russia. During my capture there, I received only two hours of rest per day, no money, no food, and no shoes. I wore two bags on my feet. After a certain time, I met two German soldiers, one of whom suggested to me an escape route.

I agreed. In Siberia it was very, very cold. We decided to wait until it was warmer. It was time to go home.

We began our trip. It took us five months without food. We were so tired, and we travelled always in silence. We were very frightened. Often, during our escape, we had to hide. When we arrived in Germany, the two soldiers stopped and I continued the trip home. It was a terrible situation at my home. No one knew me. I was excessively thin. I spoke only Russian. I was not able to speak German, but later, the language came back to me.

My mother, my two little sisters, and I went to West Germany. We took the animals, two tractors, and other things which the Germans left at the house. The trip lasted two full nights and one full day. We had no passports. If we had been captured, the soldiers would have killed us.

After two years there, I met a girl who was going to Canada. She asked me if I would like to go, and certainly I said yes. My mother and my sisters decided to stay in Germany, but I decided to go.

I eventually travelled to Montreal and got a job with a Jewish family. After a while I met a young man from Germany. We married and then honeymooned in Florida. When we got back, there were very many worries. The Québécois wanted to be the separatists of Canada. We were Germans and, in Quebec during this time, if one was not able to speak French, then one lost his employment.

Immediately, my husband, Albert, received his pink slip. His employment had been terminated. Albert went to the Department of National Defense and found work in Goose Bay. We looked for a house, found it on Green Street, and bought it. Albert had already begun his work with snow removal with the American forces.

We didn't like to live in the town because the people were afraid of our two big dogs. There was a big house on an island known as Eskimo Island. Only one family lived there. We bought the big house and moved to the island to raise a family. I was pregnant with my first child. Unfortunately, our son Nicky died in a boating accident. Our son Roland was born four years later. He is in the Canadian military.

I was always a very active woman. One night I went to bed after working a very hard and long day. In the morning, I woke up paralyzed. It was very difficult to accept. A few years later I moved to the Paddon Home in Happy Valley. Here they have a very good staff, but there is too much work for them.

My life is very different. Generally I am very happy, but as usual it is very difficult to accept that I am handicapped. I have no idea of the future, but I hope that everything goes well.

GUS "ERIC" BLACKWOOD

THE ROCK IN THE BOX

The Blackwoods of Bonavista Bay are famous for being good fishermen on the Labrador. Eric Blackwood is from this family and is retired and living in Hare Bay. When the family gets together there are many tales told over a drink. One such tale is the story of The Rock in the Box.

I'VE HEARD THE STORY ever since I was big enough to remember, and I've seen the rock.

That's the story of my grandfather, Ned Blackwood. The story is, he went to St. John's to ship his fish to Baird & Company.

Now the old man, he had a schooner that carried about 900 or 1,000 quintals of fish. He knew his schooner so well that he knew he wasn't getting the weight for the fish that was coming out. When they had her unloaded, he figured he wasn't getting the weight that he should be getting.

It got on his nerves. In those days, when they weighed the fish, the weights were all put in a box and it was locked. There'd be 112 pounds in the box.

The old man knew there was something wrong. He asked the weighmaster to see the weights but he wouldn't unlock the box.

In those days they used to wear what they called pigskin boots, big old leather boots. The old fella got mad and he up and kicked the box. He shattered the weight box, and besides the 112 pounds, out fell this rock. The rock was a pound and three-quarters or two pounds, something like that, that they had put in the weight box extra. So for every quintal of fish they were gaining about two pounds. And no doubt about it, he figured right.

The way the story goes, the old man hit the weighmaster and he went flying over three puncheons. He was in so bad a shape that they had to take him to the hospital. Grandfather got to keep the rock.

He could have sued Baird's. They gave him something, I don't know what. Anyway, they pacified him and that was all there was about it.

My Uncle Ned Blackwood was there when they were weighing Grandfather's fish. Uncle Ned kept the rock.

And every one of us, when we went to St. John's and went to his house, Uncle Ned would show us the rock. He would tell us the story of Grandfather and the rock in the box. I don't know what happened to it after he died.

A good many years ago, to get a bottle of liquor you had to go and buy a liquor book. I went to get one. There was an old fella there, a clerk, a white-haired man.

When I told him my name, he said to me, "Did you ever hear the story of the rock in the box?"

I said, "Yes, many times."

"Was that old fella any relation to you?"

"Yes, he was my grandfather."

He said, "If I had time, I'd tell you the story of the rock in the box. I was on Baird's wharf when that happened." But there were other people lined up there to get liquor books.

I never got his story. I never saw him after.

THE WRECK OF THE *PATRICK MORRIS*

THE *PATRICK MORRIS* WAS a 10,000-ton ferry. We were in Sydney, Nova Scotia, loading railcars when we got a call that the *Enterprise* was in trouble. The *Enterprise* was a herring seiner out of Cape Breton.

They were scrambling, trying to get something ready to go out. They decided on us. It was a bad choice because we were in a 10,000-ton ship and she wasn't equipped to save lives like that. It was the only thing available, so they sent us. But the *Enterprise* was gone (down) before we left Sydney. We went out in the area, and come daylight, we saw a body and we tried to pick it up.

I came on deck, daylight, when they sighted a body from the fishing boat. Everybody was out on deck.

It was a bad storm. On deck, we tried to pick up the body. We had it hooked one time, with a big hook on a line. We had it hooked by the strap of his life jacket but the strap wouldn't stand the weight if we hauled him up.

A fella Noah Moore was bo'sun on her. Noah and I were rigging a cargo net. We put weights on it to make it sink down in the water as we were sweeping.

I remember saying to Noah when the seas hit her, "Geez, this one won't stand much of that."

We didn't know that the stern door was gone. She had a docking bridge on her stern and it was 54 feet above the water.

All this time we were stern-on to the seas. The seas were like mountains. One particularly big sea hit her and burst in the stern door. When the door went she was all open to the sea.

The water just rolled into her. If the steering had stayed working, we probably would have brought her head-on to the wind and the sea wouldn't roll in there. But the water got down into the steering compartment and shorted that out. So the steering went right away. There is nothing you could do about it then. All we could do was get out of her.

It was only 20 minutes from the time the stern door went until she sank. That's coming in pretty fast when you think of a 10,000-ton ship—20 minutes.

We were the starboard boat's crew. We got one lifeboat away. We tried to get the second one away but the ship listed aport, so everybody went to the port side. That lifeboat was certified for 52 people and there were 47 of us in her. The day before that, when we left Port aux Basques, a young fella missed her, so we were one man short in crew.

Four people stayed on board the *Patrick Morris*, including the skipper.

The lifeboat would have had a full capacity. With the capacity of people it was certified for, there wasn't much room to handle the boat in a sea.

We were lucky because everybody was a small-boatsman. Everybody knew how to handle a small boat, but if we had been a crew with people from cities, we never would have made it.

Myself and Fred Wheeler were on a bow oar. There were others on the other oars. All the oars were manned by two people.

Oh geez, it was stormy. We were in her an hour and three-quarters, I think. The ships started coming but they couldn't take us. The *Ambrose Shea* came there but her crew couldn't do anything. She had a big rubber around her. If she came near us, she would have sunk us right away. She could only stand by, up windward of us, to try to give us what shelter she could.

Then this German ore carrier came on the scene. She was a big thing, a 21,000-ton ship, the *Rhine Ore*. They had the right gear to make the rescue. By the time they got to us, they had her all rigged with scramble nets and rope ladders over the side.

I'll tell you how bad it was. She was 21,000 tons and she was empty, only in ballast. They had to put her right across the seas to shelter us, and she would roll down. There were fellas who left our lifeboat that just grabbed the rail when she rolled. They never had to get in the net.

We had two old men, well, they seemed old to us, in their late fifties. We were afraid they wouldn't make it. We tied ropes around them before we sent them up the ladder. When we saw them gone, then it was takeoff! We jumped to the ladder and clung to the net.

The Germans were there, all lined up to grab us over the rail.

When we got over the rail, they took off our lifebelts and life jackets and took us to the galley. In the galley there were fellas with lots of coffee and bottles of brandy. As we came in they gave us a mug of coffee and a drink of brandy, every man.

They did a nose count. Until then, we didn't know who was not there. We knew the skipper wasn't there and we knew the chief engineer wasn't there because we saw them on deck when we hove away from the *Patrick Morris*. We got a count of how many there were and wrote down their names. The purser went to the wireless room and radioed it in. After we got straightened away they took us to the bridge to meet the captain. Two at a time, we went up to the bridge and thanked him.

The captain said to me, "Boy, don't thank me. You saved your-selves. It will never happen again that a crowd of men in a boat like that, in a sea, that somebody wouldn't panic. You saved yourselves by keeping your heads. Nobody panicked."

It was a one-time experience. One time in a lifetime was enough to do that. We had fellas there that it happened to before. One fella there, a friend of mine was torpedoed three times in the war—Lew Goulding. He was torpedoed three times and his brother was drowned overseas in the navy. It was tough on him.

The four left aboard the *Patrick Morris* were lost. All we found was Skipper Roland Penney's body.

The *Enterprise* never had a chance. She was an old wooden herring seiner, and she was built as a net tender or something during the war. Herring was big business here that time.

Anyway, we never got the body we went out for, and we lost our ship and four of our own.

MOVIE NIGHT AT BADGER'S QUAY

I WAS HOME WITH A BROKEN ARM, so I got a motorboat for going back and forth. There was nothing in Safe Harbour. We had to go over to Badger's Quay for everything, even to see a movie.

I don't know what the movie was, but a fellow named Earl Parsons used to go around showing movies then. He was supposed to be there that night showing a movie in the Fishermen's Hall.

There was a good breeze of southeast wind. When we got outside the harbour the engine broke down and we were driven ashore and the wind kept breezing up.

When my boat went ashore the sea went out and she tipped on her side. The next sea came in and swamped her. I knew I had to keep her from bouncing too hard. Ross got up on the engine house, and Bram and I were trying to hold the boat steady. I got out in the water to hold onto the boat. The only rope we had was the tiller ropes. We took that off and lashed the two girls in the boat, on opposite sides.

I had my arm in a cast. We were there from that time until twenty minutes to twelve, when we were picked up. We were waving the flashlights and bawling out. A fella who lived down the shore came out and saw our lights. He went down and told Hubert Granter, "There's a schooner ashore and fellas bawling up there on Safe Harbour Point."

Hubert figured right away who it was. "That's not a schooner; that's Gus." He went out and got Sam Barbour. Sam had a motorboat and they left and came up. When they got up to us, they couldn't get in where we were because it was blowing too hard. They went into Safe Harbour, got a dory, and came down and landed on the back of the island.

They came back out and threw a line out to us. That way we got ashore, from the little island of rock.

We were there for four hours. It was 8:00 when we left, and it was twenty minutes to twelve before they got us to shore out of it. I was standing up in the water for four hours. The cast on my arm soaked to pieces.

There was my brother Ross, the youngest fella; he was 14. There was Bernice Andrews, a schoolteacher who used to board with us, and my sister Sadie, and a buddy of mine, Bram Feltham. This was the crew.

I lost my boat and I never saw the engine after. Of course it wasn't worth any fortune. It was only an old thing I had picked up. I think somebody got it up afterwards but I never bothered about it.

There's stuff that happens to you in a lifetime.

It isn't much to write a book about.

CHARLIE BOWN

BELL ISLAND MINER

Charlie Bown was born in Newfoundland. His father came from Nova Scotia to Newfoundland to manage one of the two companies mining on Bell Island. When Charlie Bown grew up, he went to work as a Bell Island miner.

ON THE MORNING of January 17, 1938, I made my first trip down into No. 6 Mine. The previous week had been spent going to the main office to get hired on. I was given a small brass disk with a number stamped into it.

With this disk, I became only a number, no longer a name. The number would allow me to go to the company store to pick up a miner's helmet, a wide leather belt for my waist to hold my lamp, coveralls, and safety boots.

I was told the hours of work: 10 hours per day, 60 hours per week at the rate of 32 cents per hour, or $19.20 a week. I was also given a book on safety regulations.

About 6:00 a.m. on Monday morning I went to the dry-house, or change building, by No. 6 Mine. In this building I was given a line on which I could hang up my clothes. Washing materials and showers were provided when I came off shift.

Dressed in my work clothes, a helmet, a belt, and safety boots, I proceeded to the lamp cabin. Here I passed in my number and received a numbered electric lamp. It was an expensive item and I was responsible for its care.

At 6:30 a.m. all the men left the dry-house and went to the mine opening. At the opening of the shaft there were flatcars known as trams.

There was a line of about 10 trams holding 30 men on each one. We all sat with our legs inward so they could not swing out and hit the walls of the mine tunnel.

Going down into the mine, a man with a very bright light sat at the front of the train. He was the "trammer" or signalman. He looked out for obstructions such as fallen timber or rock on the tracks ahead.

At the bottom of the mine, long tunnels extended east and west. At the entrance of each tunnel there was a row of ore cars pulled by an electric locomotive. The men got off the tram and got aboard the ore cars to be taken to their place of work.

The mining process in No. 6 Mine was the "pillar and room" method. This meant a square opening was drilled into the solid ore and then proceeded inward. This left pillars on both sides for support. The wall of ore towards which you looked was known as the "face." The sides of the room were known as "ribs." The roof was called the "back" and the floor was called the "footwall."

Two men using an air drill bored 12 holes to a depth of 10 feet. The centre of the room, about 10 feet across, was drilled in a wedge affair. This pattern would have been planned and drawn out by the foreman earlier that morning. The wedge piece detonated first, leaving the straight holes to be blown out more easily only seconds later.

The blasted ore was loaded aboard four-ton cars. A machine called a "drag" hauled the ore from the face to the opening of the room. The other method was to load the ore by hand. Horses hauled these cars to the face or the room. Two men, one on each side of the ore car, would load their complement of eight cars a day, or thrity-two tons.

Locomotives pulled the ore cars to the main dumping area, known as the pocket. Another series of cars, six in number, would haul the ore to the surface.

Around 10:00 a.m., it was mug-up time. This was done in shifts as the work had to continue. Lunch at noon was done in the same way, with no stoppage in work. At 5:00 p.m. all work ceased and each man made his way to the main slope to board the train for the 20-minute journey to the surface.

I washed and changed my clothes and headed for home. My first day . . . I had become a Bell Island miner.

GORDON BRADLEY

DID JOHN CABOT LAND AT BONAVISTA?

Gordon Bradley of Bonavista is a founding member of the Bonavista Historical Society. He is a local expert on the area's heritage. I asked him if John Cabot set foot on land at Bonavista.

THAT'S ALMOST AS BAD AS THE QUESTION that one of the BBC fellows asked me last summer when they were here. They asked me what I thought Cape Bonavista looked like when John Cabot came around.

I answered, "It's like all the rest of the bloody coast. Rocks and trees!"

The new sign coming into Bonavista, put up for the John Cabot celebration last year, says: "Site of Cabot's Landing." That is a mistake.

Cabot's Landing was never the phrase that was used. It was the "Landfall of Cabot." A landfall is really where you sighted land. So you would come up to the land you sighted from your ship and search for a place to land, if you planned to go ashore.

We don't know if John Cabot ever went ashore at Bonavista.

Landfall means "the first sight of or approach to land over open water."
— Canadian Oxford Dictionary

RUBY BUDGELL

MY LABRADOR LIFE

Ruby Budgell now lives in Northwest River, Labrador. She spent her early days in a small camp on a river. Her father used the river to get to his fur traps in the interior. When his children were old enough, they moved to a village with a school.

I WAS BORN IN Nascopie River, January 5, 1924. That's where my parents were living at the time. My dad was a trapper, so I was born at the Nascopie River camp near the mouth of the river.

Father grew up in Kenemish, which is across the bay. He fished for salmon and logged, working at that sort of thing all summer. Then in the fall he went in the country. He went up to Nascopie River. My mother went with him after they were married.

There were only two families there: My mother, brother, and myself and my aunt and her children. My aunt brought me into the world. She was a midwife to Mother.

My aunt used to look after trade with the Indians when they came out in the wintertime. She was Aunt Annie McLean, married to Gilbert Blake. She was my dad's sister.

So we were the only two families up there.

We lived there until my brother and I were old enough to go to school. That was about 1929.

We had to come down the lake, that big, long lake. Grand Lake is over 40 miles long. We came down before the ice went out in the spring. I can remember, vaguely, coming down around the last year we were up there.

My dad never, ever kept a dog team in his life. He didn't like driving dogs. They always built their own catamaran. It was strong, because it had to carry everything, but it really was the frame of a komatik.

He put the family in the canoe on the catamaran and pulled it down. If we had to go in water on the ice or anything, we kept dry. We were quite young, and my mother would walk with him.

It certainly was not hard that time of the year. We were on smooth ice. We had the canoe for protection in case of holes. That lake is an extremely deep lake, so they used to pull them down that way.

We came down that spring and went over to Kenemish. We had a cabin over there.

That fall we came back here to Northwest River and bought a little log house down by the river. We stayed here that winter because my brother and I were old enough to go to school. My mother and father both were determined that we were going to go to school until we were finished, for which we can be thankful.

To me it was a break to go to school. I preferred it to a lot of other things I had to do. I really appreciated it. My mother needed help as much as anyone in this community did, with a big family. But we helped to do the work after school and on weekends.

I enjoyed school a lot. Being the eldest of the family, I had very little childhood, because there was always lots for me to go out and work at when I got home from school.

Gladys Burdett

Blackberry Wine and Ranger Mercer

Gladys Burdett was born in a small town called Aillik, Labrador. Her father was a fisherman and caught and traded in fur. Gladys and her father, James Chard, always did things together. She told this story in Cartwright, Labrador, where she now lives.

ONE TIME, IN A COOKBOOK belonging to my grandmother, Father and I found a recipe. It was for table wine made out of blackberries. Well now, we had to try that. I picked the blackberries and squat the juice out of them. We put five pounds of brown sugar with it, and so much water.

We had to put it in a tub for six weeks and bottle it off for three months. We had 12 rum bottles full. We had them sealed and put upstairs. One night, about 12:00, we heard a noise.

Bang. Bang!

I said, "Father, what is that?"

"That's your bottles."

Sure enough. Some blew up. We took them out of that and we poured them in some more bottles. If you drank an inch and a half in a glass you would feel the effect.

When people came in from the cold, Father gave them a shot of this wine. It would warm them up.

In the winter my brother was going up to Makkovik. I said to Sam, "When you go up, ask for a couple of gallons of blackberries. I want to make some more wine."

He went up and came back with the berries.

Later, I went over to Makkovik. Someone came along and said, "Gladys, Mr. Mercer wants you in his office."

Frank Mercer, from Bay Roberts, was the ranger.

I thought, what does he want me for? He must want a date or something.

I went down to his office. "Whatt do you want me for?"

He said, "You're making moonshine."

"Moonshine? Where did you get that from?"

"Uncle Billy Edmunds. I asked him what your brother wanted the berries for. He said you were making moonshine. I'm coming over tonight to test it. Have you got any?"

"Yes," I said, "I can get out a bottle. Come on over."

After I left, I said to my driver, "Bill, let's go over as quick as we can go. Frank Mercer is coming and he's after my wine."

When I got home, I said, "Father, we're in trouble."

He said, "What is the matter?"

"Someone told the ranger I'm making moonshine."

"Give me a full one and an empty bottle."

He took a full one and tipped out half the wine. Then he filled it up with strong, strong tea. Can you imagine what that tasted like?

He said, "Take the half bottle and the full ones. Go and put them in that house over there. If Mr. Mercer speaks about it, you bring out this bottle with half tea into it."

He came to our house. He sat down and said to Father, "Mr. Chard, I hear Gladys is making moonshine."

"Probably she is. I don't know what she does. Gladdy, you got any of that wine left? Get a glass for Mr. Mercer."

I brought him a glass and he poured it out. I can see him now. He took the glass and he tipped it back. "Ah, not bad, not bad."

Father said, "That's what Gladdie is making. For some old woman who got the tummy ache."

Ranger Mercer said, "Got any more?"

"Yes, Mr. Mercer. Would you like to have a bottle? You could have it if you want it."

"Oh no. You keep it, I don't want it."

That was all right. He went on and never said any more about it.

Later, the Hudson Bay Company fella came and I gave him a good bottle. I knew he would never tell.

I put this story in *Them Days* magazine a few years ago. Frank gets *Them Days* all the time. I wonder what he thought when he read it.

Life in Aillik, Labrador

MY FATHER, JOSEPH CHARD, was a Newfoundlander from Coley's Point, Conception Bay. His father came to Labrador to a place called Turnavik and from there he went to a place called Aillik, which means in Eskimo "the sleeve of your coat."

Father was brought up in Coley's Point, but he got an urge for Labrador and furs. My mother was Ethel Sparkes, from Bay Roberts. They married and they came down to Aillik for a winter.

That was about 1911 or 1912. Father started a fur business. They had no house to stay in but they got a store to stay in, something like an old shed, and later I came along. I was born in Aillik and the midwife who brought me into this sinful (laughing) world was an Eskimo woman. The only English she could say was "yes" and "no."

My mother sent a dog team seven miles to Makkovik to get another woman to interpret for her.

I couldn't speak English until I was five years of age. All I played with were Eskimo children.

There was no penicillin, nothing, when the Spanish flu hit. Out on the islands they went into places where there were people dead on the floor and sitting up to their tables. They went into one house where there was a small child. The parents were on the floor, dead. She was in the bed and there was a dog coiled right around her. He kept all the rest of the dogs away from her. They had to shoot that dog to get close to her.

Before they got there, all she lived on were the frozen redberries. She used to put them under her arm and thaw them and eat them. They took the child and put her in a room by herself and they washed her, because she was full of lice. They didn't get the flu and she didn't get it. I've seen the woman. She has been in our house. And I know the woman who rescued her.

Some women came from Indian Harbour, farther down the coast from Rigolet. They had this flu and my brother and I got it. What Mother did they wouldn't do now because it stinks too much. She took a pick of flannelette and she soaked it in the cod oil, rendered out in the puncheons by the sun. She put that on our chests and on our backs. I can imagine that smell and I can remember sitting up in bed at night with the kerosene lamp. There was a saucer with molasses in it and a few drops of kerosene oil. She warmed that and she'd give it to us to drink.

When Sir Wilfred Grenfell came back down in the winter, in February, she told him what she did. He said, "That's the only cure."

Mother said, "But I don't know what it smelled like."

"It doesn't matter about the smell. You caught it."

It saved our lives. She said I used to go blue in the face so long she thought I was gone. Just the two of us got the flu. My other brother didn't get it at all. He was out going around in the fresh air. I don't know how we got it, probably from somebody kissing us or something.

Father dealt in furs. In 1923, it was the year of white foxes, and of course the season was closed the fifteenth of April. But there was a lot caught after that. I'll say no more!

Father caught 90 himself that year and they were $20 a skin.

I was two years old when my father made three trips to the Kiglapaits. We'd go down with him for loads of fur. And we had one trip to Nain. Then my mother took me and my two brothers and my nanny, and an interpreter, and went to Nain buying another load of furs. In the morning this woman came in with a silver fox. A silver fox was worth $900.

Mother said, "What do you want for this fox? Do you want all cash or do you want to take it up with food?"

"No, no, no."

"Well, what do you want?"

"I want your baby."

Mother said, "Take the foxes and go on. You don't get my baby and I don't want the fox!"

Because I was a white baby.

It was a good healthy life. People then, they shared with everybody. Everybody was your friend. When you went to their house you didn't have to rap on the door or go in and ask for a cup of tea or a cup of coffee. It was "come on in" and "I wonder what I've got to share with you." It's not that way now.

You were always welcome. And they always had something put away for the white man—a tin of milk or some sugar, a bit of butter. That was put away for when the white man or minister came there.

MY TORN DRESS

IN MARCH THE OLD FOLKS ALL GATHERED in for a time on the weekend. We went to John Anderson's house. We put the quilts up to the window so the minister wouldn't see any lights if he passed by the house.

Of course, Mother said, "Gladys, you're not going dancing."

Father said, "Ethel. She wants to go dancing. It's only keeping time with the music."

Mother said, "No, she's not going at that wickedness."

Anyway, I went. My friend said to her aunt, "If Gladys comes out to dance, you won't tell Mrs. Chard, will you?"

"No."

I had this beautiful dress that Father brought from Montreal. No one had a dress like it. I got out to dance, and going around the table there was a nail there. If I didn't hook my skirt! Well, the dance was spoiled.

I went home and one day later Mother said, "Gladys, I never see you wearing that beautiful dress your father brought you from Montreal."

I said, "Why, Mother, I'm not going to wear that around here. That's only for special days." And I never did tell her what happened.

I was about 14.

THE MORAVIAN SCHOOL

WHEN I WAS SEVEN YEARS OLD I went to Bay Roberts with my grandmother for two years. At nine I came back. In Makkovik they had the Moravian Mission station there with a boarding school. I went to the boarding school with about 68 children. We went there in September and finished in June. They used to take children until they were 15.

At that time I thought the rules were cruel, but now I appreciate it. Every big girl had a little girl to look after, to see that her teeth were brushed and no buttons were off and no rips in her clothes. At 7:30 the little boys and girls would go to bed in their own dormitories. Then the big girls would go to bed at 8:00.

And the boys all wore suits of clothes to school.

Everyone had to go to church Sunday morning. On Saturday the big girls would take the boys' suits and press them. Skin boots with white bottoms were the Sunday boots and the girls cleaned them too.

On school days we would get up at 7:00 a.m. They'd come in the morning and wake us and we weren't allowed to speak. Sometimes we'd have to crack the ice in the enamel jug to wash our faces in. Then we all lined up in the corridor.

You'd go in and stand around the table, the boys to one table, girls to another. We would sing our grace and sit down. We still weren't allowed to speak. And you know what we had for breakfast? A cup of molasses tea, a cake of hard bread with no butter, and a plate of porridge, cooked the night before in molasses, and that was lumpy. If we didn't eat it for breakfast we had it for dinner. I used to think, Oh my. Home it was sugar, tea, and jam, toasted bread, and look what I'm eating. What am I eating this for?

But I'm glad now because I can eat anything. I can eat frozen meat. I can eat frozen fish. I can eat dried fish. There's only one thing I can't eat, and that's beans.

The Moravians had a litany like the Anglicans and they had their confirmation like the Anglicans. Their hymns and music were the same, but they were slow. They used to have a rule. The women and girls would sit on one side of the church and the men on the other side. They had two *kigoks*, that's two elders, two women on one side and two men on the other.

We had to march to church and sit up straight. If we turned around, Aunt Bertha Anderson or Aunt Susie Anderson would glare. If we did that in church we wouldn't have any dessert for lunch. We had to behave ourselves.

When we were going to school in Makkovik they got the Christmas tree in the morning, and by 3:00 all the work was done on Christmas Eve. We dressed in our best clothes for church. The schoolchildren would come out with candles. There were no candlesticks. We all had a candle stuck in a little bit of square turnip. Of course we ate the turnip afterwards! The turnip was a delicacy.

The schoolchildren sang "Silent Night." We were dressed in our best clothes. After supper Santa Claus came with his bag and gave every child a gift. Then we had our stockings hung up in the night. Christmas was a very holy day.

My brother was drowned when he was 16, off Aillik.

We don't know for sure how he drowned. He and another fella, a Newfoundland fella, went out in the morning on the ninth of October to catch fish for the dogs for the winter. They were gone a long while. Someone finally went to look for them. Someone said the last time they saw them they had their heads in the engine house. Apparently the boat broke down. Now, off Aillik Cape there's a shoal that breaks every three-quarters of an hour.

They figured they went on the shoal and the boat went over, because the top of her was all beaten off. My father went to look for them and all he saw were bits of the boat that came ashore. He came home bawling and Mother ran to meet him. She collapsed. I don't know how I got through it.

Until I was 13 I was a spoiled little brat. I didn't know how to make the bed. I didn't wash the dishes or anything. When Mother went in shock I had to go and call out next door. "How do you cook pea soup? How do you cook fish and brewis?"

The woman said, "I think Mrs. Chard cooked her brewis 10 minutes." Can you imagine brewis cooking for 10 minutes?

The nearest place to us was seven miles away. There was an old lady there and her grandson or son who stayed with us. We had a small place and I had to feed Mother. The only way I could get her to eat was, I'd take a mouthful and give her a mouthful.

When Sir Wilfred Grenfell came in the winter he said, "If you hadn't treated her with kindness she would have gone mental."

I don't know how I did it.

I was 13 the year my brother drowned. Sir Wilfred Grenfell came down and wanted young women to go and train as nurses. I wouldn't tell my mother because I knew she would say no, but I told my father I was going to put my name in.

He said, "The proper thing."

That's what I decided to do. My friend was going. They were

going to pick us up in late October to take us out to the States to train us as nurses, but my brother drowned and that was the end of that.

One spring we had money but we didn't have any food. I can't remember the date or year, maybe 1936, somewhere around there. We had the money in furs but there was no food on the coast. The telegraph office was 75 miles north and we couldn't get there by water and we couldn't get there by ice, because it was break-up time.

For two weeks we lived on salt fish boiled in water. I guess we might have had red berries from the year before, partridgeberries. We might have had bakeapples, but I know we had no bread.

One time two families came from out of the bays. They had about five children. Before that we could have three slices of bread. Mother said we had to cut down and give those children a slice of bread in the morning and a slice in the evening, or a bun. I'd go down with a little basket, quite proud, and give everyone a bun for their breakfast and dinner. I can remember that just the same as if it was yesterday.

One beautiful evening Mother said to Father, "This is the last pan of buns in the oven for the children."

He said, "What are we going to do now, Ethel?"

"Oh, by the time this is taken out and eaten, there will be something here."

As she opened the oven door and took the buns out, the old *Kyle* blew in the harbour! We couldn't believe it.

Father said, "I want to see what you had."

She said, "There's a quarter pound of sugar, a quarter pound of tea, half a pound of butter, and a tin of milk."

"Now," Father says, "what would that do?"

"Well," she said, "if someone got sick, we could give them a drop of tea with a bit of milk and sugar in it. They could survive on that for a while." If people were faced with that now they'd commit suicide, I think. They couldn't stand it.

I didn't find it lonely living in Aillik. When I got to about 13 or 14 I had my fox traps out and snares out for hares. With my gun I went shooting partridges. I had a shotgun sawed off for killing small game. I'd get up in the morning and bring home my partridges for dinner.

On my best day I got four or five partridges.

But the best day Father and I had was in April. The partridges flew south and there was what we called the Berry Banks, where a lot of partridgeberries grew. For a couple of days in the middle of April all the partridges pitched there. This morning we went up.

Father wouldn't shoot if he didn't kill four to one shot.

The next morning we went up until he was down to one cartridge. He said, "Now, look. There are four partridges there on that rock. See if you can kill the four with one shot."

Of course I did. We killed 190. And I got pictures of it somewhere where Mother got some cleaned, put on the komatik and all.

And ducks! We had 300 ducks hung up in the store. One year we had 250 seals we got right around the cove in the nets. They were for dogs' food and sealskin boots. I caught five Arctic hares. We had fresh meat all the time.

I killed a seal one day, what we called a crawler. They get up out of the ice and they can't find the water. We saw one coming around the point and Father said, "Come on, get your gun. There's a crawler coming. See if you can kill it."

Of course I went out and shot it. But Mother, she didn't want to touch it because she was afraid of guns. Not me.

I guess I must have been around 11 or 12 or 13. I'd go with Father. In the latter years I went with him all the time because he had heart failure. We would leave in the morning to see his traps until we reached his camp, seven miles away. We would stay the night and the next day we'd walk back.

Father had what they called two crews. We had so many men to go and haul the cod traps and bring in the fish, and so many ashore—to work in the stages to clean it. You put them on the table, then you have another person to cut their throats, then you pass them along to the header to take the head and guts out of them and then pass them along to the splitter. I was header. I had 40 quintals of fish one day. My brother came in, a Saturday it was. He said, "I got two boatloads of fish and if I had a good header we will have them done by 11:00 tonight."

If it wasn't finished by 12:00, at one minute to twelve, whatever was on the stagehead was all thrown away because it was a sin to do it on a Sunday. I said, "I'll come and do that for you." I went down 11:00 in the morning and 11:30 I took the last head off.

I was tired, but do you know what I had to do after that? I had to come home and scrub the floor with cork and sand because the minister was coming the next day.

You had a piece of cork and you had sand. You put a patch of water on the floor and put your sand in it. Then you would take your cork brush and you'd go over it to make it nice and white. Sometimes you used a piece of net, a piece of linnet, we called it. That would do it too. We had wooden floors and we had mats.

WINTER TRAVEL BY DOGS

WE HAD 15 DOGS. I had my own team with three or four. We had a special dog team. If customers bought more stuff than they could take, my brother took it to their homes with a dog team.

I had a dog team driver. One time I was almost caught out, me and a young fella. We went to Makkovik which was seven miles away, by dog team. We had to come back that evening, Sunday evening, because my other brother wanted the dogs the next morning.

I said to my driver, Uncle John Anderson, "We're going to leave now, Uncle John, and go to Aillik."

"Well," he said, "you better not, because we are going to have a storm."

"Well," I said, "we have to get over."

"You better not go."

"Oh," I said, "it's lovely."

We were just across the bay when it struck. We couldn't see the leader and the young fella with us said, "What will we do?"

"We'll let her go on. She'll bring us home. Father always said the dogs will bring you home." We knew nothing, saw nothing until the dogs tangled up around the woodhorse out by our door. We went in. Father said, "Where did you come from?"

"We came from Makkovik."

"Well, if I had known you were out I would have been worried."

"Well, I'm home now."

Father always said, "If you are out in a storm, just let your dogs go. They will bring you to a house, somewhere."

Father was caught out one time for six days and six nights. I don't remember because I was two years old. He was in Nain. He went down for furs.

In the morning this old man said to him, "Don't you go today. There's going to be bad weather."

Father said, "No. It's a lovely day. I'll make it all right."

"Before dark it's going to be stormy."

Father wouldn't listen to him. He went on. About 6:00 she came and you couldn't see a thing. He said his dogs started to go in towards the ballycatters—ice humps in the rocks—but he kept turning them out. If he had let his dogs alone they would have went on in to the house, because people heard him going by. They were calling his dogs in, but he kept turning them off.

He got to a big bank and took his snow knife and he made a snow house. He got in there and stayed for six days. When it got fine enough he went up on the little hill to see where he was. When he came back the dogs were tearing up his skin pants. He said to himself, "If I go asleep again, I won't wake up."

He didn't know how he got on his komatik. He tied the lash line around his waist and sat on the komatik. He went from Davis Inlet over to Hopedale. When he was going in there were some dog teams coming out.

They knew that there was something wrong with him. He couldn't speak. They took him to their house and gave him something to eat.

The next morning he got out of bed. He knew he had to try to go back home because he was all swollen. The next morning there were 11 dog teams with him. The Eskimos brought him home and he went to bed.

He asked them what they wanted. They didn't want anything, but Mother gave them grub to take back with them.

That was in April. He never walked, never made a step from April until September. His legs swelled up.

You know how Mother cured him? She said to the man we had for working around, "Go and cut a hole in the ice and get me a boiler of salt water."

She bathed Father's legs with hot salt water three times a day. That's what cured him. Just like Captain Jackman, the hero.

ARNOLD CHAFE

SEAL FINGERS

Arnold Chafe is one of the old-time fishermen from Petty Harbour. Besides fishing, he went to the ice to hunt seals.

I WAS LUCKY ENOUGH that I never got seal fingers. I often cut myself out there and bandaged it up. You often heard tell of seal fingers.

Seal fingers came from a strain. That's what they always said. When they had the seals sculped, some fellas would put a rope in them to tow them. Or you could put your fingers in where his eyes were, in the eye sockets, to pull him along. With the real heavy ones you could pull your fingers out of joint.

Seal fingers was a pretty bad infection, with swelling and pus, and it would be some sore. You could go to what doctors you liked. Old Mrs. Stafford on the Southside Road was an ordinary person, but she could cure them. Fellas I knew went to her.

You could get a cut, and then the old fat would get in there. A friend from Petty Harbour was out with me. He got two seal fingers on the one hand. He had to go up and get them done up. There were two women doing them up, to keep them dry and everything.

The two women bandaged them up, and then they hauled a condom down over the fingers. There weren't too many of them seen in Newfoundland, but that's what they put on them, a condom. When he came back down, the boys said to him, "What? They did them up with condoms?" They couldn't believe it.

There were a few fellas who said, "Well, they weren't brought out here for that reason, but they come in handy!"

ARTHUR CLARKE

AMBULANCE DRIVER

Arthur Clarke was born at St. Thomas, Conception Bay. In his youth he fished with his father before finding work outside his home town. At Bell Island, he eventually was hired as a driver of the ambulance, which was in those days, a horse and cart.

I WAS SENT TO BELL ISLAND when I was 17 years old. I got a job down in a little mining pit called 44-40. Then I went to another surface pit, where I carried on for years. From that I got a job down in the East Barn, shovelling snow for the big bosses.

One day I was asked to go teaming horses. I went down just for the day. When I had the day in, the boss told me to come back the next day. He said, "Half the boys down here won't take the horse you got because they're afraid of it."

The horse was called Ben. When I would back in for coal, he would start to dodge off somewhere. I began to give him extra oats at the start, and another handful when I finished. After a while, that horse never moved. All the rest of the crowd were afraid for their lives of him. After that, whenever I went in the barn, he would bawl out to me. He knew my scent.

That's how I got in the barn. Dinner hours most of the boys used to go home. If anyone had an accident, I would go to wherever there was trouble.

I used to be a doctor, chauffeur, and undertaker. Not just me. Some of the other boys there in the barn did the same thing. Sixteen of us worked there.

After a while, they got a square wagon for an ambulance. It was all open. It puts me in mind of those chuck wagons you see on TV sometimes.

They had a horn on the outside of the barn. You could hear it all over the place.

They would call the barn and tell us where to go. Then I would put the harness on the horse and go. By the time I got the call and I reached No. 3 Mine, it would take five minutes. To get to No. 4 Mine, the farthest one away, it took 12 minutes.

I drove out in the open, not covered. There used to be hard winters those years. With the wind in from the north and the snow squalls.

I was at that for 26 years. In those 26 years I saw some queer, horrible accidents. Some of them lived and more of them died. I saw people burned. Burned to death.

When I brought them to the stretcher, I thought I would get half sick.

I witnessed men coming out of the mines after a fall of ground. One man was six foot two. Two and a half tons of stuff fell on him. His body was flattened, and he was hanging out over the sides of the stretcher. I saw some horrible old accidents, wicked.

They later hired out the ambulance job to someone with a van. I had to do something else. I didn't like the mines job. I saw too many accidents, to tell you the truth.

I got a job as a blacksmith's helper. I was there for five years. Then, when there was a maintenance helper off, they put me at that.

I started off at 28 cents an hour. I used to bring home $16.80 for a 60-hour week, 10 hours a day.

RHODA COLLINS

I LOST MY LOVE FOR SCHOOL

Rhoda Collins lives in a comfortable house in Glovertown. She is a religious woman, and full of wonder at the good things around her. The following is an excerpt from Mrs. Collins's book on her life, *He Was There All the Time.*

TO ALL MY CHILDREN: Greetings in Jesus's name. I am now at the age of 77. Twice a widow and now living alone. Yet not alone, because God is with me.

I thought it good to write a story of my childhood days to keep on record for you. Most of this you will find hard to relate to, being brought up in a different age.

I was born and raised in a small place called Silver Fox Island. My parents were Job and Maggie Rogers. I had three sisters: Eva, Statia, and Priscilla, and one brother, John.

Childhood days were exciting days. I loved going to school. I liked helping my mom around the house. I was the oldest child and felt responsible to help. My sisters and brother grew up the same way.

I have a sad memory of the last day I went to school, which I have never forgotten.

My father spent a lot of his time away from home. He went down to Labrador in the summertime, or was away getting firewood, cutting logs and catching rabbits in the wintertime.

Wintertime we would have a lot of snow. Sometimes it would be up over our heads. Mother would work so hard shovelling it. First she had to clear a very long path for us to go to school. Then she would have to clear a path to the woodshed, the drinking well, and the clothesline. Then she would take a break to prepare dinner for us children, who would come home hungry as bears.

In the afternoon she would go right back shovelling again. She would make sure it was all cleared before another storm came.

We would have fun sliding over the hills in the snow and making snowmen. Evening we all had our chores to do. I would get two one-gallon cans and fill the water barrel, which had to be filled every day. Then the woodbox had to be filled and kindling had to be prepared for lighting the fire in the morning. Mother would light the fire and warm up the place before calling us children up. Sometimes our bread would be frozen. We would put it in the oven until it got hot and then put butter on it. It would be delicious.

I loved my father and hated to see him working so hard. He would have to bring firewood up over the hill on his back. I would help him saw the wood with the old crosscut saw. Later we got a bucksaw, which was easier to use. There were no chain saws in those days. My dad would cleave the wood and my brother and sisters would pack it in the woodshed. The shed would be filled, making sure there was enough for all winter.

One day at school I took very sick. I tried to walk home but only made it halfway and couldn't walk another step. My sister stayed with me while my brother ran home and told my parents. Dad came and picked me up in his arms and carried me home.

Each day I got worse. Dad went to Greenspond and brought the doctor. He said I had rheumatic fever and had to have total bedrest. Mother brought my bed down to the kitchen where she could be with me all the time. I grew worse and couldn't feed myself. After a month I could stand but my feet were still swollen.

Our minister, Rev. Sheppard, came to visit me one day and encouraged me. I wanted to go to school so badly, even though I could hardly walk. I was determined to go, so Mother would dress me warm and pack a lunch. I would go to my Aunt Lizzie Hunt's house, which was near the school. My brother and sister would pull me on a sleigh to and from school. How I loved to be back in school again. It wasn't long before I was back on my feet.

Our first year of school was primer class, where we learned about animals and their names. Then we went into grades one and two. The only books we had then were the Royal Readers and an exercise book. We had a slate and learned to add, multiply, and subtract. We had bookbags to carry our pencil box, slate pencils, and water in a bottle, with a cloth to clean our slates. One morning I was so disappointed. My water was frozen and my pretty little bottle had broken.

Sometimes we would carry a couple of pieces of wood to school for the wood stove, our source of heat. School days were exciting. Sometimes the harbour would freeze over and we would walk across the ice, which was a much shorter way.

We dressed warm, with our knitted caps, mitts, and socks. There were no slacks for girls, but we had spats to pull over our boots and button up the sides. We also had fur muffs to put our hands into.

The last year I went to school, new books came out. I bought them all. Geography, Hygiene, Arithmetic, and Grammar. I was excited about my new books. There was so much to learn about the outside world. All the different animals, the beautiful people, and so many things we never heard of before.

We grew up on a small island in a little world of our own. There was no communication with the outside world. We had no radio or telephone in those days. There was so much to learn from our new books.

All was going well for me until one morning, our teacher Baxter Norris did something very foolish. Just after school started that morning, he discovered the name "Joseph Matthews" written on the window sill. He asked who did it, but everyone denied writing it.

Each child had to go up to his desk and take an oath on the Bible. Still, nobody did it. Then each child had to write Joseph Matthews on his slate, to see whose writing was most like it, so he could judge the guilty one.

I hadn't seen the name on the window. However, he judged my writing to be the one most like it. I knew I was innocent, but as a sensitive child, it was too much for me to take.

It was dinner hour and my heart was breaking, so I left the school, never to return. So that's how my school days ended. I have suffered much for it over the years.

I went home from school that day and broke down crying as I told my mother I would never go back. She was hurt as well, but didn't force me to go back. We all thought the teacher had done a very foolish thing.

It took me a long time to get over my hurt. I lost my love for school, and was deprived of my education. I always liked to do things well, but for the education part, I will never measure up.

My writing is very poor and I am unable to do the things I would love to do. However, I've tried to pick up what I can, on my own. I have come this far, thank God, and I'm sure I'll make it now, to keep in touch with each of my family.

We looked forward to Sunday. It was our feast day. Saturday was a day of preparation for Sunday's breakfast, dinner, and supper.

Hard bread was put in soak, salt fish cut up and soaked, and salt pork cut up and fried. That would be for breakfast. Vegetables would be peeled and cleaned for dinner, with rabbit, bird, or fresh pork, and for supper, tarts and cakes were made on Saturday. This was a tradition all through the years on our island. I kept it up long after I got married, but gradually left the old tradition behind.

We used kerosene lamps in those days, one in each room. They were filled and trimmed each day before darkness came.

Sunday morning, the church bell would be ringing. After breakfast, dishes were done. We dressed in our Sunday best and off to church we would go, as happy as could be. We were taught the Ten Commandments and the Lord's Prayer. At the age of 10 or 11, we were ready to be confirmed by the laying on of hands by the bishop. Then we would receive our first Holy Communion, the bread and wine as commanded by the Lord.

MEMORIES OF SILVER FOX ISLAND

I REMEMBER MOTHER MAKING SOAP. She would save all the fat from the table until she got enough. Then she took ashes from the stove and poured boiling water on it to make lye. She added salt to it and put it outside to cool and harden. Next morning she would cut it into cakes and put it on boards to dry in the sun. It would be stored in the attic to be used for washing clothes and cleaning floors.

My mother used a large wooden tub and a wooden washboard to wash clothes in. Sometimes in winter the water in the well would be low and she had to melt snow for water.

We bought Sunlight soap to wash ourselves with and to do the dishes. There was no liquid detergent those days. Everyone did the best with what they had and no one complained.

In later years there were large galvanized tubs and glass washboards. Small children could bathe in the large tubs. For adults, a large earthen basin and matching jug would be kept on a washstand in the bedroom, for sponge baths.

My favourite pastime at night was to help my mother hook rugs. My father would make a rug hook from a fork or large needle. Then he made a large wooden frame.

Hard bread and potatoes came in burlap sacks. These sacks would be ripped apart, hemmed, and laced onto the frame. Strands of burlap would be barked for colour and a pattern of choice would be marked out on the rug. Some patterns were done with pretty colours from white material we had dyed. When it was finished and taken off the frame, it would be beautiful. There was no carpet in those days, but the bedrooms and hallways were covered with hooked rugs.

Once every week, on a good day, the rugs would all be rolled up and taken outside to be dusted. I would do the rugs while Mother cleaned the floor before we put the rugs down again.

We were always helpers. When we left home we were well trained and knew how to keep house. I thank God for my parents. They worked very hard to provide for us children. When I became a teenager, I wished many times I could earn money to help them, but it was not possible. Some people were much worse off than us. Some children I know had to wear patched clothing, but we always had shoes and nice clothes.

In late summer or fall my father would arrive home from Labrador. Sometimes they had a full load, but other times they had only half a load. It was very disappointing for them because they had worked so hard.

The fish was taken to St. John's and shipped away. When they returned from St. John's they brought back our winter supplies. This always depended on how much fish they caught. We always looked forward to Dad coming back from St. John's. We were sure he would have something for us: a few oranges, apples, and candy as treats.

Many precious souls never made it back from St. John's in the fall. There would be terrible storms at sea and many a schooner went down with all the crew lost. It would be heart-rending to all.

When I was a little girl, my father's brother Uncle Chris got lost in a storm. He was married with a wife and two little children. They were living with us at the time, and he had promised to bring me a doll when he returned. Their schooner was lost with all on board. I remember the terrible time my father went through. He was broken-hearted and no one could comfort him. It seems he took it harder than anyone else.

Another man from our island, Thomas Button, was lost on that boat. Their bodies were found and brought home to be buried.

Christmastime was a very exciting time for us. We looked forward to it with joy. All work ended on Christmas Eve. Our traditional supper that day would be watered salt cod and molasses raisin bread. Even today I like the same on Christmas Eve. It brings back pleasant memories.

After supper our tree was hung and trimmed and stockings hung. Before 9:00 p.m., we would be in bed, anxiously awaiting next morning to see what we received in our stockings. Next morning we would run downstairs and bring our stockings up. We found candy, apples, sometimes grapes, and candy canes.

We would look at our tree all trimmed with fruit. Figs and apples would be dangling down. Best of all were the beautiful, big heart-shaped candy. It was so tempting to us, but we had to wait out the Twelve Days of Christmas when the tree came down before we could eat the fruit. We wouldn't dare disobey our parents. Finally the day would came and we enjoyed eating all except the big candy hearts. They had to be carefully put away for next Christmas.

The last night of Christmas we would hang our stockings up again for another time of excitement. We were truly thankful for whatever we received. The children of today are bored and unhappy even though they have so much.

Christmas was 12 days of fun for everyone. We all went from house to house to share in what we had.

Sometimes we would dress up in old clothes, cover our faces, and go mummering. We knocked on doors and asked, "Any mummers in tonight?" In some houses we would dance, anything to make fun. There would be a soup supper and concert at the school and we'd have homemade ice cream.

There was no drinking and very little smoking in those days. I never saw a girl or woman smoke. That would have been a great disgrace. Once I saw a man get sick from drinking, after a soup supper. I became very frightened and fainted. My parents had to take me home.

We had a nice dinner on Christmas Day, but never turkey or chicken. Maybe ducks or pork. We raised our own pigs.

Mother made sure we had a new garment to wear on New Year's Day. That was a tradition as well. We always had special clothes to wear to church but were not allowed to wear it any other time.

As a child, I loved to visit my grandfather at Newport. My grandmother died before my mother married. Mother was their only daughter and they had a son, Uncle Elias Collins. Later, my grandfather remarried. I knew and liked my stepgrandmother. My father's parents died before I was born, so I didn't know them.

Grandfather Collins would often come up to my parents' home to visit. He always brought me something: a doll, a cap, or candy. He gave me so many little things I appreciated very much. Of course I was his first grandchild, so I got all the attention. When I got older I used to go to Newport to visit Grandfather. I loved his house. There was something special about it that still brings back good memories that I shall never forget.

Uncle Elias Collins married Aunt Jane. They had a family and all lived at Grandfather's house. I can still picture my grandmother putting her white flour-bag tablecloth on the table, and her beautiful homemade bread. With roasted cod and homemade jam, it would sharpen the appetite of any child.

Pancake Day, the beginning of Lent, was a day we looked forward to. We knew what we would have for dinner that day. When we got home from school there would be a large plate of pancakes on the table. Each one had something inside it, such as a ring, a button, or straw. Each was supposed to mean something. The child who got the ring was going to be married first, the button meant a seamstress, the straw a good housekeeper, the nail a good carpenter. I must have gotten the nail! The person who got the nickel was supposed to get rich. We all wanted that one.

The next day, Ash Wednesday, we went to church, morning and evening. We also went every Friday all through Lent. It was a solemn time when everyone was supposed to fast from something. There was no activity during that time, not even a marriage. On Good Friday nobody would work or cook a meal. We wouldn't even throw water outdoors until after sunset. Saturday was a solemn day as well, thinking of our Lord's death, but Sunday was a day of rejoicing, remembering the Lord's Resurrection.

Eggs were a treat for us children. We had a couple of hens and sometimes we watched them to find out where they laid their eggs. We were sure to save up enough so that everyone had one on Easter Sunday morning. We boiled them and put them in egg cups.

Of course, Easter Monday was a big day. There were soup suppers and teas, and dancing at the schoolhouse.

Valentine's Day was another day we enjoyed. We didn't send cards like children of today. Our tradition was to make a request for something in the form of a rhyme. We didn't ask for anything big, just small things, as we knew we were more likely to get them.

I used to watch my mother making bread and begged her to let me do it. She wouldn't, but one day I went to Newport to visit my Aunt Elsie. She was in her sickbed and needed bread made. Her children were all younger than me, so I offered to make it. I placed the pan on a little chair and made my first bread. I had a problem putting it in the pans and couldn't see how I could manage it. I did my best and the children enjoyed it anyway.

Summertime we would play outside. We would cover the top of the woodhorse and make a tent. We would chew hard bread and make cakes from it, then enjoy eating them.

Wintertime I would watch my father knit or mend nets. Sometimes he would make a casting net for casting capelin. We used capelin for fertilizer on our gardens in the summer.

Dad and Uncle Bill would build boats together in the wintertime, either motorboats or rowboats. The rowboat had a sail and, depending on the size, paddles or an oar. When the wind was in the right direction you could sit in the boat and have a nice time along.

Sometimes I would watch Dad and Uncle Bill saw plank with a crosscut saw. One man stood in the stage while the other stood up in the stage loft, and they pulled the saw up and down until the planks were sawed. When the boat was built, it was caulked and painted. It was fun watching the boats being launched and given names.

The motorboat had an old-fashioned engine. Before I got out of bed in the morning, I would hear the boats all around the harbour, with the click click click of the engines. Everyone was on the move as soon as the ice moved out in the spring, getting their firewood home. It had been cut in the winter and hauled out by rope and handslide to the shoreline, ready to be loaded aboard the boat in the spring. Sometimes they would tow a small, full boat behind. They had to have enough to last until fall. It was hard bringing it all uphill to the house and sawing it up and packing it away.

The women would be busy in spring also. Most everyone owned sheep. They would shear the sheep, wash, card, and spin the wool. There were plenty of mitts and socks to be knit, making sure everyone had enough for the winter.

Everyone had vegetable gardens. Before starting gardening, they had to take the sheep away, as no gardens were fenced. Names were put around the sheep's necks with leather name tags. Then they were loaded into boats and taken over to Indian Bay, where they were free to feed all summer. In the fall, after the vegetables were up, we'd go back for the sheep. Sadly, many of them were never found. The last one I had after I married was never found and I never got another. We would cut grass in summer and make hay to feed the sheep all winter.

Summertime we went berry picking. We would walk in a little path to the upper end of the island. Blackberries would be the first to get ripe. We got lots of them to keep Mother going, making cakes and puddings. After that it would be raspberries, red currants, and blueberries, enough to keep us busy all summer. Mother would go to the marshes to pick bakeapples and bottle them. They were delicious for desserts, lasting all through the winter.

When I got older, I joined up with a crowd and we would row over to the main shore to pick bakeapples. We would be gone all day, especially if they were plentiful. We would light a fire and boil the kettle on the beach and sit down for a big feed of smoked salmon and homemade bread. Some people on the island had smokehouses and smoked salmon all summer long. We enjoyed our trip and our feeds, making sure we got home before dark.

I remember the first trip I had away from home. My mother took us up to Glovertown on the steamer. It was at night and as we were coming up the bay a little bird flew down in the cabin. That caused quite a bit of excitement.

Mail was carried by the steamer, both in Newfoundland and Labrador. To send a letter to someone on the Labrador, it had to be addressed to the person, name of the schooner, in care of Labrador Afloat. If they chanced to connect with the steamer, they got their mail, but if not, they would be gone all summer without a word from home. If there was a death at home the steamer would raise a black flag.

If there was a telegram for anyone on our island, a flag would be raised on a pole at Fair Island. Someone would go up in boat to get the message. Often it wasn't for the person who went for the message, but there was much co-operation among the people. The mail boat brought our mail and we loved to see it coming in the harbour.

To get the train we would go by passenger boat to Gambo to connect with it. My first trip on the train was when I was about 12 years old. My mother went to Fair Island with me, where we met with Caleb Ackerman, who was going through on the train. I was going to Glovertown, so she put me in his care.

All my teenage years I spent away from home. The first summer I spent at Traytown with Uncle John and Aunt Florence Littlejohn. Aunt Florence's family were all grown, so she wrote Mother and asked her to let me come and spend the summer with her. The following summer I came back to Traytown to work with the Kean family.

When I was 15, I went to Glovertown to work with Aunt Jane Holloway. She had four sons at home but was unable to work. She was a dear lady and each day would manage to get downstairs and sit in her chair. She showed me what to do. I would wash, cook, and clean for them. People were so limited in those days, with no jobs and very little money. I remember I got $5 and bought myself a nice grey coat. I was so pleased with it, and later got enough to buy a pair of white sneakers.

Aunt Jane taught me how to card and spin sheep's wool. I knitted socks for the boys. That benefited me much in years to come.

The next time I left home it was with my parents. They moved up to Lockyer's Bay to cut logs. I spent one night with them. The next day I went to Hare Bay and got a job with Percy and Nellie Wells, who owned a business and took boarders. I earned $5 a month. I stayed for six months and went home in the spring.

Transportation from Hare Bay wasn't easy. I knew the Matthews brothers were at Trinity building their schooner and would be going to the island on the weekend. I decided to go Trinity and go home with them. There I met Walter Matthews, who became my boyfriend and later my husband.

Later that spring I made up my mind to do something I never thought I could do, because I didn't like being on the water. I was always seasick. Father was going to Labrador with Uncle Bill Wicks in the *Polly Bee*. They needed a cook and asked me to go, so I decided I would go. I thought that I might meet up with Walter some time during the summer, but I was in for a big disappointment. His crowd was home a month before we got back. We left home the first of July and arrived home the sixth of October. It was a terrible long trip, and unusual to be that late getting home. We were over a month on the water. Everyone at home was worried and wondered if they'd ever see us again.

It was not all hard times, though fish was scarce and we only got part of a load. We went down as far as Mount Pike.

One day, it was a beautiful morning and all the men from our schooner and the schooner nearby had gone out to haul their traps. I didn't know anyone lived near where we were, but we saw a boat coming toward us and heard men talking. The girl on the other schooner was just as scared as I was. Two dark men were coming right for our schooners. I didn't know what to do.

First they went to the back of the schooner, I guess to see her name. They were talking loudly in their own tongue. They could speak some English, and one man came over talking to me. He asked where I was from, and my age, and then asked me to marry him. I was scared stiff and didn't know what to do. I had bread baking in the oven, but I was afraid to go down to take it out. They had a loaf of dry bread and jug of water in their boat. They kept getting down in their boat to break off a piece of bread. I knew they were hungry, and if I hadn't been so afraid I would have given them a meal, as I was taught to be kind to people. I had never seen a black man before, and I guess the fear instilled as a child came forth.

As children, we were told not to tell lies or the black man would have us. That meant the devil. We never questioned the old people, but I did fear the "black man." I'm sure it was this fear that so terrified me. I didn't even know there were coloured people in the world at that time.

We came up to a place called Ford's Harbour and I came in contact with Eskimos again. I was on the schooner alone this time also. I heard them come and was still very much afraid. I had heard that Eskimos didn't like heat, so I went down in the forecastle and put lots of wood in the stove, hoping the heat would drive them away.

Two women and two or three men came aboard. They went back and forth, looking at everything they could see. Then the old man came up to me and asked my name and age. I told him, even though I was almost too scared to speak. After that, a woman came over. They admired my hair. "We all black hair," she said. I was wearing a red skirt. They admired red and wanted so much to have it.

I knew they were hungry, so I invited them to have some pea soup I had cooked. They couldn't stay long because it was too hot for them. They brought a pair of beaded slippers and a little purse made of sealskin, which they wanted to exchange for some clothes. I looked among my clothes and gave them all I could spare. I really enjoyed my fur slippers and have never seen like it since.

The first of July, when we left home, it was a beautiful day. We planned to have fish and brewis for supper. When we were coming in to Seldom the wind changed and the schooner listed on her side. The pot with the fish and brewis came off the stove and over the floor. I didn't cook under sail anymore. I was too seasick for that.

We got caught in a terrible storm that came on suddenly. I was down in the forecastle and couldn't get back to the cabin, where I used to stay under sail. The storm didn't feel so bad back there. However, I climbed up in the top bunk and held on for dear life. Every time she took a nosedive, water came into the forecastle. It took two men pumping constantly to keep the water out. Every man did his best to get back to land. Every now and then I heard someone shout to ask someone to check on me to see if I was still alive.

We had been out in some high winds and heavy seas, but that storm was the worst. The *Polly Bee* was very old. She had no engine and they had to depend on the wind. When it came the wrong way it would be tough going, and when it was calm, sails were no good. They would put out the motorboat to tow the schooner. You can imagine how far we would get in a day with a small boat towing a big schooner. When we crossed the Strait of Belle Isle, it was so calm the men put the oars out and started rowing. We all looked forward to that wonderful day when we would reach home. Each day brought us a little closer. We never despaired, thinking of the joyful reunion we would have with our families who were anxiously awaiting our return. My boyfriend was also anxiously awaiting.

Tears of joy were shed that sixth day of October when we sailed in the harbour. Mom had a beautiful supper prepared for us, with bakeapples for dessert. To meet up with my boyfriend that night was an experience of homecoming one could not forget.

Uncle Sam Wicks's wife had a new baby the day we came home. So after spending one day at home, I went over to help my aunt take care of her family for a few days.

I was hoping to go to St. John's in the fall, but it looked hopeless for me. Our schooner had been so late getting home, and it would be very late before they had their fish ready to take to St. John's.

However, the *Silver Jubilee* had been home early, and ready to take their fish in. It would be the first trip to St. John's for the *Silver Jubilee*, and a couple of the Matthews women were going and asked me to come along.

I gladly accepted and we had a very enjoyable trip. I worried about Dad and the crew of the *Polly Bee* having to travel so late in the fall. However, God took care of them and they made it back safely.

I was married to Walter Matthews at the age of 18, in St. Andrew's Church on Silver Fox Island, on June 5, 1936. We didn't have much of this world's goods or a big wedding, or large gifts as people get today. But we loved each other, and love covers it all. I remember the day I walked down the church aisle with the man I loved. I felt like the happiest person in the whole world.

MILDRED CRANFORD

One job many young girls found around the bay was to go in service to a minister or merchant, or any other persons who could afford hired help. In 1925, Mildred March of Green's Harbour came to New Harbour in service with Harry Cranford, a widower left with a child to care for. Harry's parents, Uncle John and Aunt Ann Cranford, along with Allie Smith, completed the household.

For Miss Mildred March "in service" meant more than just doing housework, and she remembers.

IN SERVICE

IN SERVICE, AROUND THE HOUSE, since Mrs. Cranford was sick, I had to do everything. I worked in the stage, on the flakes, in the gardens, and I had to do the housework too. When I came here [June 2, 1925] Mrs. Cranford had all her wallpaper and paint and varnish bought to do the house with, and before Mr. Cranford [John] came home from Howley that fall, I had all the housecleaning done, the painting, the papering and varnishing, myself.

Then 'twas carding and spinning; we had six sheep. Knit that up then, stockings, mitts, vamps, drawers. That's what Mrs. Cranford was at the fall I came here, so I learned from her how to knit drawers. That [drawers] was something to put in the washtub and scrub on the washboard. Heavy? My poor little hands used to ache. Every bit of strength would go out of them.

The water was low in the well. Poor Harry made a hoop for me; and I'd take up two galvanized buckets and the hoop and go up to the culvert and bring down so many turns of water for to put in the big water barrel for the next day's washing. The culvert was in the big brook up there, up on the track.

In service I also made blubber soap. All the fat you'd save would go to make blubber soap. Any fat on your cookin' water, you'd strain off, and scraps of fat you'd save up until you had enough perhaps, to make a boiler of soap. You'd put it on, let it boil, then throw in the Gillett's Lye to make it thick like jelly. You'd take it off and put it to one side to cool. You'd cut it out then, in cakes. You'd have your lye soap for cleaning with, and Sunlight soap for washing your face with. If you had a bit of Sunlight soap to wash yourself for Sunday evenin' service, you was all right.

COOKING ON THE LABRADOR

Many young girls also found work cooking for fishing crews on the Labrador. From Grandmother Cranford comes her story of her only summer on the Labrador.

I was 14 when I went down on the Labrador, in 1919, to cook for six men. In our crew, beside myself, there was Albert March of Green's Harbour, his son David, Mr. Ernest White, Caleb Pitcher, and two fellows from Hopeall, a Piercey and a Cumby. We got the schooner in Harbour Grace on June 1 and came back in late October. We weren't the only crew that went down. Poor Father went down with Captain Noseworthy, who owned the schooner we went down on. They went to Snug Harbour. Our crew and the Yetmans' crew went to Tug Harbour, except the Yetmans were on the shore, and we were on an island out from them.

Where I was on the island, there was a great big house with a wharf front. When I was there, what a state the house was in! I started to cry. There was nothing to do nothing with, in a place like that, and the men comin' in and nothing clean. I felt some bad. I was 98 pounds when I went on the Labrador. I was that small, Father used to call me "cock emmet."

The first thing I did when I went there was clean up the house. The supplies, the salt was all in Snug Harbour, and came to Tug Harbour in motorboat. I'd get up 5:30 or 6:00 to cook breakfast for the men. I'd cook bread puddings, pease puddings and potatoes, salt beef, fresh fish, baked beans. For mornings, we'd have baked beans some days, rolled oats porridge others. There was only rough grub then. Uncle Albert March didn't like me to use sugar in my cookin', trying to save on expenses, but I found my sugar anyway.

I used to have three shifts of clothes one week, three shifts the next. I'd wash for three men one week, three the other week, and I'd darn their stockings and their cuffs. In the evenings, every day, I'd bake bread. Just imagine turning out 11 or 12 loaves of bread a day. Then the washing, and if I had spare time I'd work on the beach making fish. I didn't help with the men when they got back in the evening with their fish. I had enough to do. The only work I did with the fish was making it on the beach, if I had any spare time. 'Twould be late when I got to bed, depending on when the men got back, usually 6:30 or 7:00. First they'd have supper before getting at the fish. I wouldn't go to bed until they finished the fish and I got them a lunch.

On the way up, or down, I don't know which, I got sick. There was one man on board, he was some nice. Anyway, he killed a couple of small birds and made some soup, and brought me some. When we came home in the fall, we were loaded down with fish. I was down in what we calls the hold. All that was facing me was bins of fish. Now, the young girls was down there, and by and by, I see the young fellas crawling in too. Well, I got frightened to death, because I was young and didn't know what 'twas all about. I was scared. Anyhow, poor Father came down to see how I was and I told him. He went and told the skipper, who put me in his cabin.

I shipped down for $40 for the summer. When I came back in the fall I bought a tam for $2.50 from Aunt Jane March's shop. The tam was green plush with a red band and a black tassel . . . I thought I had my fortune when I got that tam. The rest of the money I gave to Father to help get a bite for the winter.

JOHN "JACK" T. DOMINIE

I SURVIVED THE WRECK OF THE SS *CARIBOU*

Jack Dominie was born at Cape La Hune, on the west coast of Newfoundland. Here is his story of the wreck of the Gulf ferry SS *Caribou*. She was struck by a torpedo in the early morning of October 14, 1942.

I JOINED THE *CARIBOU* on the first day of August, when she was in St. John's for a refit. We signed articles to sail on the twenty-seventh of September and picked up our run in North Sydney.

My job was seaman. We were on watch the night she got torpedoed. Those times you had four hours on and four off. Now, we were on at 12:00 that night. Well, we had to get up and let the other watch go off. I went on watch on the starboard side of the bridge that night.

Captain Tavenor was coming and going all night, one place and the other. I don't know how many different men he sent up on the wheelhouse, to see if they could see the lights from the escort. He was an uncomfortable man.

We didn't get any warning. Two o'clock I went in and took the wheel, and that's where I was when she got torpedoed.

I left the wheel and started to go down on the starboard side. I couldn't see anything for steam. The lifeboats were all covered in with steam, where it struck the engine room, I suppose.

I got to the starboard side and met the bo'sun coming back. He said, "Boy, it's no good for you to go over there. Everything over there is all tangled up." He was excited. He was looking for his young fella and he was all excited.

But anyhow, I went on over. The lifeboat was there, but I couldn't see it. There was a big crowd of people in the boats, and others trying to get in. We never had much time to do anything. There was a fella there, a passenger. I told him to hand me the axe. He handed me the axe and I chopped the belly bands on the lifeboat.

I didn't know what to do. You couldn't lower a boat that was full of people like that. Myself, I only had a last chance. I thought now I'll get into her myself. So I got into her, and I sang out to someone, if any of them had a knife aboard. They said they did. "Now, when I call out cut, you cut."

So that's what he did. And we made a great landing on the water. She dropped down even. A great landing on the water. This was No. 4 Lifeboat. She was filled with people, with no standing room in her.

We were not very far when the *Caribou* sank. I would say perhaps 20 yards. She filled full of water. It seemed like the water was running forward in her. That's how she settled, by the head, and when she got down far enough, there she went, headlong.

THE PLUG WAS OUT OF HER

IT WAS NO TIME before the lifeboat was full of water. I went to check. Those times, the plug was supposed to be out of a boat when she was swung out from davits. Whoever made that rule, I don't know. Nobody would ever make that if they knew what they were doing, to keep plugs out of boats that were used for emergencies.

I dare say that might have been all right if she was just a cargo boat, with just the crew. But when you had a load of passengers, that was something else. I tried the best as I could to get the plug in, but I couldn't get it in.

Where she was loaded with people, the force of water would blow it back every time. So, before I'd get a chance to drive it down with my foot, it would be back out.

I did that, I don't know how many times, and I thought to myself, it's no good for me to do that, because she's filling with water.

So I took a bucket then. I started bailing. Well, that was foolishness, but we didn't know what to be doing, see. I said, well, that's it, it's no good for me at this. I wouldn't say we were in her 10 minutes before she was filled with water and started to roll over.

So that's what happened. She filled full of water and rolled, and the people all went into the water, the poor women and children, all of them. It was dark. There was one woman alongside me, I could see her with a baby.

I don't know how many times she rolled over. When she finished rolling, there were just a few of us left in her. And when we were picked up there were only the four of us.

I stayed with it, lucky enough. I got knocked clear of her once, but not for long. I couldn't swim, but I propelled myself alongside of her again. She was rolling back and forth, face up and bottom up. There was a lot of wind, boy, that morning. A lot of wind.

Our second cook was one of the survivors. And I know one of the fellas belonged to Neils Harbour—Jack Hatcher. He was another one that survived it. The other fella was American, I think.

I knew all the crew members. They were all from Port aux Basques, pretty well. Israel Barrett was in the watch with me. He went to call the new watch, and he wasn't gone five minutes before, Bang!

I figured that he never survived. He would be back in the galley, boiling the kettle for the crew coming on. I figured that on his way back he was handy to where the torpedo struck her.

Our escort, the *Grandmere*, took us aboard. They looked after us. They gave us dry clothing and everything we needed. They took us to Sydney, where we stayed that night, and the next day we returned on the SS *Burgeo*.

Luck was with Jack Dominie in the years ahead. He served on two other Gulf ferries, the William Carson *and the* Patrick Morris. *These two also sank, but Jack was not on either of them at the time!*

I am sad to report that Jack Dominie has passed away since 1998 when I interviewed him. — G. Cranford

CYRIL DuBOURDIEU

SHIPWRECK AT PICCADILLY

Cyril DuBourdieu lives in Port au Port East. After a career in the Canadian Army, he returned home to retire. While going to school as a young man, he often joined ships to act as a Newfoundland customs agent. On one occasion he was shipwrecked in the middle of winter.

IT WAS NEW YEAR'S EVE, I think it was, when we drove ashore in Piccadilly. I joined the SS *Fernfield* in Sandy Point. I would get off her when she finished up in Port au Port Bay. From there she would leave to go on to Bonne Bay.

It was 1943. At that time there were no roads on the peninsula here at all. All the freight was delivered to the various stores around the peninsula. Abbott & Haliburton was the company that owned the stores.

It was before Confederation and everything had to be checked in, because of duty being paid. Fish and so on being exported had to be checked the same way. There was an export duty on it. For that reason you had to have a tidewaiter on the ship going around the peninsula, before she was cleared from port here to go to Bonne Bay.

I used to get out of school at that time to do the tidewaiting duties for Newfoundland customs. Twenty-five cents an hour. Of course you got it from the time you joined until you got off, 24 hours a day.

The Wind Came up Pretty Heavy

WE HAD LEFT CAPE ST. GEORGE then, at Three Rock Cove. Then we went in to Piccadilly to land another bunch of freight—apples, flour, salt beef, and kerosene. We were unloading when the wind came up pretty heavy. The ship started to disintegrate at the pier that we tied up to.

We had to move away from the wharf. All the crew that were on the jetty just slipped our lines and let us back up to anchor. We went out and anchored. Once we anchored, everybody went down below to relax. Twenty minutes later the ship started to bounce on the bottom. We were right up on a shoal. By now it was midnight.

The bottom was sandy and the anchors didn't hold. She drove right up on what they call Piccadilly Head, a rocky shore. The biggest problem was the loss of power when the engine room got flooded.

In fact, I almost lost an arm in it. We were down in the galley getting a lunch after we anchored, and when she brought up on the bottom the partitions started to move inside. My elbow slipped in between the partition and the side of the ship. I had to wait for it to roll back again in order to get my jacket out of it.

The First Boat Smashed

THE ONLY WAY TO GET ASHORE was to lower a lifeboat on the capstan. There was enough steam left on the boilers to do that. The first boat went in and smashed up against the big ice wall on the shore.

They lowered the second one, and that's how we came ashore. But I had to jump in the water up to my waist and claw at the ice pack. Everyone got ashore, but clear of a few bruises, nothing serious happened.

We were frozen when we got ashore. Of course, all these ships carried a little bit of black rum. Everybody went up to a rooming house, the staff house owned by Haliburton. Most of us stayed in there. Mrs. Duffy was the person looking after the establishment.

The ship didn't really break up that night, but later she started to founder, and fell apart. Afterward, there was an awful lot of pilfering because she was loaded with freight. Of course, it was all insured.

She was a total wreck.

HOWARD ELLIOTT

BIG GAME OUTFITTER

Howard Elliott grew up in big game country. He was born in Millertown, on the shore of Red Indian Lake. Before starting hunting camps, he was an equipment operator for the Anglo-Newfoundland (A.N.D.) Company.

IN 1958, WE STARTED A HUNTING CAMP. Claude, my brother, and myself. I did the cooking and everything and Claude did some guiding. He had just one year at it, but I stayed with it. I was the first one with a guide licence in Millertown.

The A.N.D. Company had hunters coming to them, but they had no place to keep them. I was on the river at the time, and Ed Ralph, our woods boss, wanted us to take a camp.

He said, "Howard, whatever you want, from a fork and a knife to a D-4 tractor, it's right there for you. It's only a matter of going and picking it up. Use away until you get it paid." That's where we started off.

I bought it off the company for $1.07. Seven cents was tax.

My main camp was at Lake Ambrose. It was a former A.N.D. Company depot. The carpenters and boatbuilders and other workers stayed in that building.

That year I started off, I had 78 visitors. They all stayed at the camp. I had thousands of room.

Every weekend we'd have hunters. Then we started to spread out, until I had 17 guides. I had three cooks and my wife. I had seven speedboats, a tractor, a J-5. I had four pickups, outboard motors, and everything. The boats were for the rivers and the different lakes.

Our Long Lake camp was big, 52 feet long. That was a nice lake, Long Lake was. A rough lake, just the same. It was about half a mile wide, and when you got out in the middle, the water was rough. One time I had to go right to the bottom of the lake and turn around and come back on the other side. We couldn't get across it at all.

My three main camps were at Lake Ambrose and Long Lake, and one down in Stratton's Valley. I could keep 15 at Stratton's Valley and 21 at Lake Ambrose. I had another place for the guides to stay in, down alongside Red Indian Lake, alongside the Exploits Dam.

MOOSE COUNTRY

MOOSE? DON'T TALK, FOR THE LOVE OF GOD. From Lake Ambrose down to Exploits Dam, that was 15 miles. I've counted as high as 60, 70 moose. You'd never believe what you'd see.

We had 38 hunters there one week. They came on a Sunday, and by Wednesday evening we had everybody packed up, ready to go home the next day. Not a soul left without a moose or caribou.

The best area we had up there was Stratton's Valley. We used to have 16 hunters there, and every week we'd have our moose. We came out one morning to bring the moose out, on a Thursday or Friday. From the camp to the road, we counted nine moose in five miles. That was after we had taken a lot of moose along that same road.

There was no end to it. Moose were all over the place. The woods were just cut out by loggers, and they were right into the browse.

NORMAN GABRIEL

I CALLED THE WILDERNESS MOTHER WILD

Norman Gabriel is of Mi'kmaq Indian descent. He had a difficult time as a little boy. Now in his late eighties, he pauses and speaks in a hushed, hurt voice when he remembers the racial prejudice he lived with in Stephenville, Newfoundland.

MY FATHER, Alphonsus Gabriel, died young. I was five years old. I think he did a bit of fishing and a bit of farming. I was born in January, 1910, or 1911. My mother's family was from here. My mother was a March. Her grandmother was a Mi'kmaq, with the last name of White.

Because we were Indians, I was treated like the plague. When they'd talk about poor Dad, they would spit and say "Indian!" like it was a dirty word. Nobody wanted any part of me. I had no friend that would help me in any way.

I had a teacher up there I'll never forget. I was singled out by the teachers. They had a stick to hold up the windows. That's what they used to crack us on the knuckles.

Some of the boys used to pick on me and I used to fight back at them. I had no choice, I was all alone.

To people in those days, I was always Indian. As I got older, people respected me and talked to me. The feeling of being alone and ashamed was not as bad.

An old man, Henry White, took me under his wing and taught me the ways of the world. He was 50 years old when he started trapping, in the woods. Trapping and hunting for big game, in the winter.

Henry White treated me like a son. God rest that man. I hope he went up to Heaven, because he went for the underdog like I do today. He saved my life.

The year I went to go in the country in the winter, the trees opened their limbs and welcomed me. In the wilderness I was home. I called the wilderness Mother Wild.

Isolated by the rest of the world, I had to have somewhere to go. How many times I would sit in the nighttime and think, and there are still times it fills my eyes.

I would go by the river. I fished for salmon and I'd sit by the river. What was it like before the white man? I liked to think about the Beothuks.

There was a crowd in Corner Brook, like me in those days, when there was no hunting licence. We'd take a moose or two and we wouldn't waste anything.

If we went to the river and the river was full of salmon, we took one or two, whatever we ate ourselves. We didn't waste. We were our own conservationists.

Now my wilderness home is gone. I long for the trees and the days I was alone.

I witnessed prejudice all my life, because I'm Indian.

MARGARET GIOVANNINI

OUTPORT NURSE

Margaret Giovannini was an English nurse who came to Newfoundland to work in the outports. Today she is an independent senior of 98 years, living in St. John's. She loves to talk about her years living in outports. Here she shares some of those memories.

I ARRIVED IN NEWFOUNDLAND on April 16, 1939. I had always wanted to travel but could never afford to do so. When the opportunity arose to work as well as travel, I liked it. We travelled to Newfoundland from Liverpool, England, on board the SS *Nova Scotia*. Department of Health and Welfare nurses met me at the boat in St. John's and I was taken to the nurses' residence at the Balsam Hotel.

The first few days were spent mainly attending clinics at the department headquarters which, at that time, was in the basement of the public library. I had misgivings about doing dentistry, which was required in the isolated outports. However, after receiving advice on procedures under the guidance of the dentist present at those clinics, I felt a little more confident.

I had been a Queen's District Nurse in England and was well acquainted with district work. I was also a certified midwife and had practiced as such for several years in England.

My first district in Newfoundland was Rencontre East in Fortune Bay, which included eight other settlements. These could only be reached by boat. It was always possible to answer calls except in stormy weather, which fortunately did not occur often.

Harbour Breton was the nearest medical centre and Dr. Paton

resided at the hospital there. One week prior to taking up my post in Rencontre was spent in Harbour Breton meeting the medical officer. We were informed on procedures to be taken when medical advice and assistance was needed. If we needed urgent medical assistance, the hospital ship *Lady Anderson* was at our disposal and answered all our calls, weather permitting. A doctor and nurse were on board the boat at all times.

Our telegrams for assistance or advice were given priority by sending a pink telegram form, which was sent immediately to the doctor on board the ship. When in a settlement on an emergency call, the doctor would visit other patients requiring attention or advice at the nurse's request.

I always looked forward to the arrival of the hospital ship as I could visit the staff, have one or two meals with them, and enjoy their company and discussions.

Before starting work on my own, I helped with clinics on the *Lady Anderson* all day. I was then taken ashore to begin my work at Rencontre. I had a busy first day, as several children needed attention. One or two were very sick.

The doctor on board the ship had already advised me regarding drugs and treatments. I was glad of this advice, as many of the drugs had different names in England.

I had a very comfortable boarding house where every kindness was shown to me. Especially in winter, if I had been away all day in other settlements on monthly visits or on a sick call, my landlady, Mrs. Baker, kept a lookout for the boat. She would have a nice big fire ready to warm me up, as well as a nice cup of tea and a meal.

A very convenient surgery and waiting room were provided. All instruments for dentistry and minor surgical needs were supplied by the Department of Health and Welfare, as was a liberal supply of drugs. No effort was spared to provide the supplies, which were ordered once a month.

All liquid medicines were provided in one-gallon jars. In winter especially, it was necessary to order a large supply, as weather often delayed the boat's arrival and no roads connected the settlements.

DOROTHY GOODYEAR

THE LOST AND FOUND TEETH

Dorothy Goodyear of Grand Falls worked all her life in a caring profession. She worked as a nurse and nursing administrator. She is well known in her community for writing many stories about her life.

IN THE FALL OF 1939, I was home from St. John's for Christmas, with my mother and brother, in our little village in Notre Dame Bay. It hadn't improved much since I left because there was not much work or money on the go.

It was what was referred to as the Dirty Thirties. But we young people didn't seem to mind. Everyone in our little place seemed to have plenty for the winter and was happy enough. Now, we all skylarked with our old school chums, just like we did when we were youngsters. For fun, I'll call one of them "G."

He was a young man about my own age. He was in our house every day and night, singing and playing.

This evening, he ran in on his way home, out of the woods, to see if my brother and I were going to the concert that night in the Orange Lodge. It was getting dark. John, my brother, was feeding the animals, and Mother was gone to the harbour to visit her brothers. When G. was on the platform, leaving, I pushed him for fun and he grabbed me around the neck.

I said, "Oh my. My false teeth is knocked out."

We put down our hands on the step as we thought to pick them up, but they were not there. Now, we were afraid to walk, for fear of treading on them. Well, we looked every inch over, and over again, but still no teeth.

Now I was in tears. My small wages in St. John's, on which I had skimped to buy them, were wasted, to say nothing of how bad I looked with four front teeth gone. I shone the old flashlight until the battery died. Then I got the lamp from the kitchen. G. lit the old faithful lantern, got a hammer, and took up the board to see if they slipped down through. Still no sign. I was heartbroken—so was G. We hoped that it wouldn't snow that night, so I might find them in the morning.

I called off the concert. I couldn't go with a mouth like that. I wouldn't have the heart. I got John his supper, fish cakes I had fried earlier. He said I had no right to be carrying on.

Poor G. left to run home, around the shore, a couple of houses away. He was heartbroken and blamed himself. John was sitting down to his supper and I was trying to mumble down a bit too.

The old porch door came open, and then the kitchen door with a bang, and in ran G., beaming, his fist clenched up, and shouting, "I got 'em, Dolly, I got 'em."

When he opened his hand, still full of myrrh, there were the teeth—hooks gleaming. I said, "Where? Where, G.?"

He said when he was taking off his bib overalls to wash and have supper, they were hooked in his sweater and were well anchored.

Many a gift has been put in my hands that I have been thankful for—even my diplomas—but never one that meant so much as the teeth at that time of no money.

We are both senior citizens now, and he has lived his life in St. John's with a lovely wife and family. They visit us in Grand Falls, where I married, and we still sing and play. When we go to their home in Manuels, we love to talk over our young days and that story is always told. I have had a lot of dental work done since then, but I still have, with many other treasures, the little teeth that nearly broke our hearts and almost made me miss the concert.

I always say now to Mr. G., "God Bless the bib overalls and the fluffy homespun sweaters."

And like little Tim, "God Bless us all."

A CARING LIFE

WHEN I WAS IN MY EARLY FIFTIES I was nursing in a hospital in Newfoundland for a couple of years. I knew a lot of the older patients from when I worked there years gone by. We were all glad to see each other again, although some of them were very sick. I did everything in my power to help them. On one occasion I came near to getting my orderly and myself fired.

This night I was doing the four-to-twelve duty shift on the male wards. All those who were well enough were let go home for a few days at Christmas. In one of the four-bed wards were two elderly gentlemen whom I knew well, and two younger gentlemen. One of the older men knew his condition and said it may be his last Christmas, but he was always so cheerful.

The two younger men were not as serious. One had his leg in a cast, the other one recovering from an operation.

On this particular night the young orderly and I went in to do them up at 9:00 for the night, as was the rule. The young man was playing a beautiful waltz on his accordion. We laid down our things. The orderly and I danced around the ward, getting great applause. Then the player changed the tempo to a fast jig, so we stepped it out, swinging each other. The other three patients were clapping and cheering us on and one of them hit the floor with his walking cane.

All of a sudden the evening supervisory nurse came in. She was mad and gave me the worst tongue-banging I ever got in my life. She said, "I don't blame the orderly. He is young, but you are old enough to be his mother and should have better sense."

She said, "You will go to the office tomorrow at 4:00 p.m."

I said, "Yes miss, with pleasure."

One dear old soul spoke up and told her that he had heard of people losing their jobs for treating the sick poorly, but never for cheering them up.

I said, "Don't worry. She is not from Newfoundland and she hasn't heard our ways yet." I told them I was cheering people up or cooling their fevered brows before she was ever born. I did not talk back to the supervisor in front of people, as we were taught better.

The next day we appeared at the office. I spoke for both of us. I said, "As you are aware, this is not my first Christmas working in hospitals. I will admit, maybe we were a bit noisy and should not have been entertaining the patients without the permission of the supervisor. We promise if we get the chance again, we will be quieter. One other thing. I would say to this nurse supervisor that I have never been belittled in front of people, as there is a time and place for everything."

We waited for the verdict. All we saw were a few sly smiles. "Go on and get on duty. There are new patients in."

The supervisor was asked to stay behind in the office. I don't know what went on, but she was as nice as pie to me after that and it was never mentioned again.

We would split our sides laughing about it and the staff would ask us when was the next free show. The dear souls welcomed us on the wards, and we had many a little step after that but were never taken to task about it. That nurse went back to her own city in the spring to get married, so she said.

I was there at the hospital the next Christmas. My two dear old friends were not with us. They had passed on and the wards were again filled with other people in need of care. In time the good orderly took another position and I returned to Toronto to carry on my work there for another few years.

THE LITTLE SEALSKIN BOOTS

LAST WEEK I WAS ATTENDING AN AFTERNOON TEA and sale of handmade goods. It was a joy to behold. As I viewed the Christmas table I thought, "Is it possible we are so near another Christmas and I am another year older?" Then I saw a little pair of sealskin boots to fit a child of two or three years old. It was a beautiful piece of handiwork.

Although I was surrounded by crowds of people, my mind went back to the late 1930s. I was working in a hospital in an outport of Newfoundland as a nurse's aide. Christmas was kept to the fullest for 12 days in the old-fashioned way, with school concerts, adult concerts, and plays. People did a lot of visiting, walking many miles through the snow to see their friends. Carol singing was big, and of course everyone attended church. There were two or three cars there, but they weren't used in the winter. So the horse and sleigh or dogsleds were ways of getting around.

As older people know, wages were very small and things were cheap. Everyone made do with what they had and seemed to be happy. No radios or televisions then, but it was so cozy sitting around the kitchen stove, the kerosene lamp giving off its soft yellow light.

We staff were all very happy at the hospital. No one went home for Christmas but stayed and cared for the sick and made them as happy as possible.

As in every outport, mummering was the highlight for young and old. We girls from the hospital used to go out with friends. One night we planned to meet at our friend's house and dress up. We took the grey and red blankets off our beds and took white rags from the laundry to put over our faces. There were eight or nine fellows and girls getting ready when I saw Mary's pretty sealskin boots, a gift from Labrador. They had grey fur with pretty red binding and bows. She had worn them on a few occasions.

She said to me, "You can wear them tonight. If I do, they will know me."

I put them on and capered about the kitchen.

Soon we all hit the snow-packed road. I fell down as soon as I made the first step on it. The crowd helped me up. I slipped, then down I went again as they walked ahead. "Wait! I'm killed!"

But in their glee and hurry to get to the first house, they really didn't think I was in much trouble. I was way behind. I caught hold to the fence and got in the house late and stepped it out to the old accordion and mouth organ music.

Then it was up the hill. It was great fun for them to see me hit the road like a ton of bricks. Someone would drag me up again. I had to walk in the snow to my knees to get along. The many falls were taking their toll on me and I was getting tender from head to foot, my old blanket dragging in the snow. But with the beautiful moon shining down, it was everything you could ask as a perfect Christmas night.

After I had gotten along to five houses, I had to retreat and get back alone to Mary's, where we had dressed in the beginning. I met some little mummers of about 10 or 12 years old who helped me back, but I was so much taller. I even knocked them down too. What a relief it was to reach the house. The sealskin boots were a thing of beauty, but I had never tried a pair before and didn't know how to walk in them.

I finally made my way back to the hospital, as I had to go on duty 12:00 and do the midnight shift until 8:00 a.m. That was a hard night on me. I was tender as a boil all over, lucky I didn't break any bones.

The next day I was black and blue, but I went mummering many times after that. With my old trusty gaiters on I could dig in my heels and keep up with the others.

Many years after, in the rush of big cities where mummers were never heard of, I thought of home and that peaceful night and the sealskin boots. Then I knew the meaning of what my Uncle Jim said. "My sealskin boots are as slippery as if I had two bottles on my feet!"

THE CHRISTMAS CAKE STAND

WHEN I WAS ABOUT 10 OR 11 YEARS OLD, I used to spend a lot of time minding my aunt's baby girl Nellie. Today it is called babysitting. Her husband was a fisherman, as most of the men in the outports were. That summer the men did well with the fish, so before Christmas my aunt gave me enough pretty plaid for a dress. My mother made it and I was proud as a peacock.

My uncle also gave me a dollar. Two shiny 50-cent pieces. I had never had that much money before and I felt rich.

I asked my mother if I could spend it and have what I wanted for Christmas. She said, "Yes, but don't lose it or waste it, and save some." Off I went to the store that had everything from a needle to an anchor.

 This was the first buying I had ever done. I bought a pretty, large cake stand for my mother, 50 cents; one hanky, five cents; one large red and green Christmas bell, 10 cents; one pack of crayons, 10 cents; two slips of embroidery thread, five cents each; three large barrel apples, one cent each; a bag of common candy, two cents; and three two-cent stamps. My total was 96 cents. I tied the other four coppers in the corner of my hanky and gave a cent each Sunday at Sunday school for collection.

My mother used the stand for special occasions. When I was married in 1946, my mother said, "You take it, my child, and use it."

Well, it did get used in my home, at church times and weddings, and was loaned out many times. It spent many years in Toronto with us. I'm happy to say it looks just as nice now as it did in that little showcase in the store.

I remember the kind man wrapping it in brown paper and tying it with twine. There were no plastic shopping bags then. He said, "Be careful, maiden, it's slippery, and mind you don't break it."

That store is gone to make way for the highway and the kind merchant has long gone. That was the day when a dollar was hard to get, but you could get a lot of things with one.

After I returned to Newfoundland I had a visit from a dear lady. She was looking at this and that. She said, "Dorothy, that cake stand must be old. How beautiful!"

Then I told her the story about it. She then told me a story I had heard many times before from my mother. She went to school to my mother at about age five or six. My mother had a gold watch. It was the style then to wear them on a cord or chain around the neck. She forgot it that morning and she asked her little pupil to go home and ask her mother for it. She said she felt happy to do so.

In the afternoon my mother gave her five cents. She was overjoyed. She wanted to spend it, yet she wanted to keep it, her first earned money. Her father stuck it to a pin and made a brooch for her. She became a famous schoolteacher herself and often told her students that story.

A CHRISTMAS BROOCH

*"Silver bell, silver bells,
It's Christmastime in the city."*

I REMEMBER WHEN THAT SONG FIRST CAME OUT. Everyone was singing it, and it is still loved the world over.

Like everyone, my husband, Tom, and I were getting ready for Christmas in our apartment in Toronto. Just as the Christmas before, I had volunteered to work Christmas Eve and Christmas Day in the hospital so the young mothers could be home with their children, as I wanted to be with mine some 25 years before.

It was Christmas Eve, everything was decorated, and in the afternoon we sang carols on the wards. A lot of the patients were allowed to go home for a couple of days.

When 4:00 came I was off duty. I had a couple of boxes of candy given to me by the staff, but as every year I stopped off to see Aunt Becky, from Newfoundland. The family had lived in Toronto for several years. Everything was ready for Christmas there, but the family was not yet home from work. She was sad because one of her sons had made a mistake and his father told him not to visit for Christmas. He lived in another part of the city and Aunt Becky was heartbroken.

In the meantime, in the hour I was there the young man took a chance and came for a few minutes, bringing Aunt Becky a gift of money and a handsome brooch.

She was worried. How could she explain the brooch when she wanted to show it and wear it? She said, "Dolly," as I was called, short for Dorothy, "can I say you gave it to me?"

I said yes and to put it with the box of candy I had given her. We tore off the tags and I wrote "To Aunt Becky With Love" and put it under the tree with the other gifts.

Then I ate a big piece of dark Christmas cake. Her dear son went through the back door and I went through the front. We went our separate ways, saying, "Merry Christmas."

I had to be at church for the Christmas Eve 6:00 family service. Big flakes of wet snow were falling like feathers. The sidewalks were slippery and the old streetcar chugged along, crowded.

Like the others in the choir, I struggled to get into my old wine-coloured robes, the smell of the hospital still on my uniform. I jammed on my choir hat that was always too tight.

A baker came from across the street, rushed in and pulled his gown on over his white uniform. The smell of the bakery was lovely on him. Soon we were walking up through the church carrying our candles, singing "Silent Night."

As the service was nearly finished, we were kneeling around the rail, the lights twinkling on the Christmas trees and the soft music playing. The people from the body of the church were coming forth to join us.

I felt someone's hand on my arm. I thought it was one of the members, but I looked into the face of a timid-looking lady in her little fur hat. I recognized her right away. I took her hand and whispered, "How are you feeling, Mrs. Brown?"

She said, "Fine, thank you. I was in the city for my checkup and I got a good report. I'm going home on the late bus tonight. I heard the church bells and came in for the service. I sat in the back, but when I saw you and knew you, I had no fear of coming to the rail. I remembered when I was so sick, and you sang for me, 'Just As I Am, Without One Plea.'"

Yes, this was the same lady who was so sick and pale, with red hair and with freckles that stood out on her dear face. She had trusted me then and was still trusting me now. I wished her a Merry Christmas and good health. Then more carols were sung and I was on my way home again.

Later that night, Tom and I did a little last-minute shopping. A man was singing "O Come All Ye Faithful." He had had one too many to drink and he was dragging a Christmas tree, top-first, into the streetcar. By the shape it was in then, there would not be much left of it if he ever did reach home.

At home the turkey was made ready and we would eat it Christmas Day for our supper. Later that night our son John phoned and said it was a beautiful Christmas Eve in Newfoundland with lots of snow.

Soon my head was on the pillow, waiting for an early rise to take on Christmas Day duties. I was not like the children wondering what would be in their stocking. That was too many years behind me. As I was drifting off to sleep I fancied Mrs. Brown's lovely face with the red hair and freckles. Mixed in with my thoughts was Aunt Becky's sparkling brooch. I thought, "Dear God, I hope the good I have done for others this Christmas Eve will atone for the lie I told about Aunt Becky's brooch."

Then I thought how clean the snow must be in Newfoundland. I knew it was peaceful there tonight, as when I was a child. I must have gone to sleep.

The next thing I heard was a sound like bells. Could it be Santa Claus coming to me? Then I realized what I heard. It was the timepiece alarming. "It's 6:00. Time to get up."

I turned to Tom and said, "Merry Christmas, dear."

WHAT IS A FATHER?

FATHERS COME IN ALL SIZES AND SHAPES, from very tall to very short. They can be very young or very old and many different colours. They live on all parts of the earth. Some have even been on the moon. Most are breadwinners who take pride in their homes and families and are loved and honoured in return. That is why every year the third Sunday in June is kept as Father's Day.

One dear father often comes to my mind. One year in the 1960s my husband and I were returning to Toronto by the beloved old train when we met a fine gentleman. He was going to western Canada to spend the winter with his son. He was a retired railroad man and was much older than us at that time.

We chatted about many things. He told us about the hardships they had to go through in the snowstorms on the mainland and in Newfoundland. Wages were not very high, but he was glad to be working when so many men couldn't get a job. One evening we were sitting in the dining car. On the table was a large bowl of fresh fruit. He looked at it and said, "I never eat a grape. They make me think of my little girl I lost."

With tears in his eyes, and ours as well, he told us of one terrible snowstorm in Newfoundland. He was away from home working with the railway when he received word from his wife their little girl was very sick.

He tried to get home by rail on a speeder. The winds blew louder and the snow drifted higher. The mother told their little girl, "Daddy will soon be home."

The worried family and friends were afraid the girl would not last. They thought she had slipped into a coma, but she roused and said, "Daddy is coming."

He told us he stamped the snow off his feet on the snow-covered platform and went straight to her bed. She put her little arms around his neck and said, "Daddy, I waited for you. Don't leave me."

He had a few grapes in his heavy coat pocket for her. They were not easy to get in those days in Newfoundland, especially in the winter.

The grapes were frozen like little balls of ice. He put a couple in her little hand and she was contented. An hour or so later, kind friends unlocked the little arms from around his neck and laid them on her bosom, for she had gone to join the other little angels in heaven.

It had happened so many years ago, when he was a young man in his prime. It was a very touching story coming from a man of his age. I have thought of that fine father and his few precious grapes and his love for his children. Many years after, I saw farmers harvesting hundreds of acres of grapes in California. I wondered if some of them would be sold in Newfoundland.

CAPTAIN WILBUR GREENHAM

TURRING IN TWILLINGATE . . . OVERBOARD!

Captain Wilbur Greenham had many jobs in his life. This is one of many stories about his life as a cod fisherman, sealer, lumberman, and captain of schooners and ferries.

TWILLINGATE IS A GREAT PLACE FOR TURRS. Me and poor old Father, we have gone out when I wasn't very big. I'm not very big now, certainly. We were in the row punt. We rowed down to what we call the Lower Head, about three or four miles. It was nothing then to come in with 60 or 70 turrs.

My brother Fred, he's still living, he was out with him, the fall that they turned the boat over. Fred was back at the engine.

Fred asked me if he could have the three-quarter gun. They had my gun and he had two breech-loaders, and out they went. He was only a young fella.

Down came three or four turrs, and a big lop on, too. Fred pushed the tiller right across her. Over goes the boat! And the two breech-loaders, gone. As for my gun, I wasn't troubled if he lost that one or not.

So all right, she's gone bottom up. Father's pipe came out of his mouth. Fred, a young fella, was a bit more active than Father.

Fred got up on the bottom of the boat, and there was poor Father in the water. He was near enough that Fred had him hooked by the fingertips. It so happened that a fella by the name of Eric Young was not too far away. And Eric came, got them in his boat, turned Father's boat upright, and towed her in.

NOT TOO LONG AGO / 67

That's all right. They went over and went in the house. Mother was there.

She said, "What's the trouble?"

He said, "We turned the boat over. The first time in my life. Mother, my dear, come on, hurry up, give me some dry clothes and something to eat."

"Why do you want to hurry for something to eat?"

"We're going out again."

That's true. She got him some dry clothes and something to eat.

He said, "Mother, I've lost my two breech-loaders. I've got to go over now and get a new one." So, he went over to see John Loveridge. He didn't know anything about Father turning the boat over. John Loveridge was running the business over there, and John and Father were the best kind of friends.

He said, "John, I need to get a breech-loader. We had a misfortune. We turned the boat over. My first time. I lost my two breech-loaders."

"Well," John said, "Skipper Andrew, if you're going to buy one breech-loader, I'm going to give you the other one for nothing."

"That's up to you."

So he bought one breech-loader and John Loveridge gave him the other. No more than an hour from the time he was in the house, got a lunch and dry clothes, he was out in the same spot again!

Tough, wasn't he? He was 85 years of age and had salmon nets out in Twillingate Bight. They had big grapelins, 70 and 80 pounds. He pulled in the whole lot, single-handed when he was 85.

No matter if it was flat calm, he wouldn't go out without putting a rope around his waist and tied down somewhere in the boat. He always did that, when he went out single-handed. The way he put it, if he fell overboard and drowned, they had a better chance to get his body. And he lived to be 93.

Father's name was Andrew, but everybody called him Chum. Chum Greenham.

RALPH HARVEY

I JOINED THE NAVY

Ralph Harvey was born in Boswarlos, on the Port au Port Peninsula, in 1917. In 1939 he went to war by joining the navy. Here is his account of meeting the Wolf of the Atlantic.

THERE WASN'T MUCH WORK around here, very little. There were just a few months' work at the limestone quarry. So I decided to join up and got in the navy. That was in 1939, the third draft.

I went with a horse and sleigh to Stephenville Crossing and from the Crossing went to St. John's by train. I boarded at a Mrs. Dawson's, until I got a ship and went over in convoy and landed at Liverpool.

The barracks were in Devonport. We did a good bit of training there and then we joined a ship. I joined her in Belfast, Ireland. The name of the ship was the *Laurentic*.

The second trip out, we were 310 miles off the northeast coast and got torpedoed. A sister ship to ours got torpedoed too, the *Patroclus*.

I was just turning in, undressed, and bang, she went! That awful smell. I wasn't long getting out of my hammock. I grabbed an old army coat and put it on.

There was no warning whatsoever. Her gun went off, and when we all rushed up on deck, there she was, right across from us, not very far. We couldn't get at it, because when we got the first torpedo our ship listed. She listed so much that we couldn't point our guns right to shoot at her. They had us, all right.

The captain of the German U-boat was Otto Kretschmer. He was so successful sinking ships that he was nicknamed Wolf of the Atlantic. He was the first to get the Iron Cross, for sinking so many tons of British shipping.

Every hatch on our ship was full of empty drums. When she got the first torpedo, all the drums started to come up through the hold and floated all over the sea. She took a good while before she went down, because the drums were keeping her up.

We were in lifeboats. You lowered the lifeboat the best way you could and then went down the lifelines. I was in a leaky lifeboat, with five or six buckets going!

It wasn't blowing, but there was an awful heavy swell on.

There were a good many of us in the boat, and there was a big steward there. He weighed 18 stone. I caught the lifeline to haul the lifeboat in so he wouldn't drop in the water. But he let go about eight feet up and he came down hard. He struck my leg and he drove my leg back. Don't say I didn't have a bad leg. I was some mad.

I said, "My son, if there were only you and me in this boat, you'd never see the shore!"

Oh my, oh my, what a night, what a night!

That happened about ten to nine on Sunday night. It was a good while before the destroyer came to pick us up. It couldn't pick us up right away, because it had to make a broad circle, around and around, to make sure the submarine wasn't there waiting. We were picked up just at the break of day.

There were two Newfoundlanders and one Englishman lost. Roy Beverley McLeod and Francis Roche were the Newfoundlanders lost.

They brought us in to Greenoch, Scotland. When we got in there, the Salvation Army was there with clothes and everything for us. Boy, I was some grateful. They were really good people. The next boat I joined was the *Prince Leopold*, in combined operations for two years, doing hit-and-run raids. And I took part in the Dieppe raid.

PEARL (BRUSHETT) HATFIELD

TIDAL WAVE: ADRIFT IN A HOUSE

Pearl Brushett lived at Kelly's Cove, Burin Island, when the tidal wave of 1929 struck. She was five years old when a wave took her house out to sea. Her mother, Carrie Brushett, and five children were in the house. It was a ride they would never forget.

THE FIRST WAVE took our house from Kelly's Cove beach over to Bartlett's Island. It grounded there.

My sister Lillian and I were in the same bed. She had an earache. Mother warmed up a plate and put it under her ear in order to get relief. Lillian still has the old plate.

My older sister Lottie said to Mom, "Are you going to wake up Lil and Pearl?" Mom said yes and she came and woke us up.

The first thing I remember after they woke us up was looking out the window. All the flakes and all the stages were down in the harbour. The harbour was all debris. I remember that.

Then the second wave came and took us back to the beach. Not exactly where it came from, but near. That's when Mr. Ben Hollett and his wife, Beatrice, came down and got us out through the parlour window.

The windowpane was 12 by 24 inches. That's what we all went out through, that pane of glass. Mom cut her wrist when she broke out the glass. My sister Lottie jumped out and she got a big scar on her right forearm.

I don't remember being scared. Mom was there, so naturally we figured Mom was going to look after us.

Lottie and Mom went to Mrs. Hollett's house and got their cuts bandaged. Years later, Mom still had pieces of glass coming out of her wrist.

Then we took off and went higher on the hill, which they called the Humpess Head, but don't ask me how it was spelled.

I remember the next day. I know it snowed, because I remember Fred. He didn't have any clothes to wear. I can see him so plain, in this child's dress. We were down helping pick up some of the debris and found some of the girls' dresses. I guess they were from the neighbours' children.

Our house didn't break up. It was towed in and moored off in Ship Cove by the old schooner *Daisy*.

THE CAT WENT WILD

EVEN THE OLD CAT STAYED IN THE HOUSE. It got really wild. When they tried to get it out of the house, it jumped out the window and over someone's head and swam ashore. We never saw it after. It probably just went wild.

Dad was down in the woods, cutting wood for the winter. I think it was a couple of days before he heard. I remember him telling me their boats all went dry, down there in the bay where they were. I guess they were laying down or something and they heard all the chains rattling because the tide was all out.

Dad towed the house back to Kelly's Cove. We used to use it for a fish store, where we stored the salt fish.

I had nightmares for a long time after. In my dream I was always going up a hill and the water was only a few feet behind me. For years after. I was traumatized, I guess.

After the tidal wave, Mother always had a roaring sound in her head, like the sea. She never, ever got rid of that. She lived until she was 75. She always heard that noise. I imagine she was in shock and she was never treated for it.

You know, floating around with five children in the house, I guess you would be in shock too!

WILSON HAYWARD

Food Aplenty!

Wilson Hayward is one of the best fishermen in Bonavista. The first few times he went in boat, he got sick. The next day he would cry to go out in boat again. To him, work was fun and he loved every minute he could get on the water. He says no one went hungry in Bonavista, unless they were lazy or in poor health.

I'LL TELL YOU WHAT WE used to do in the fall of the year. My father would go fishing in the summer right up to September month. Then he would take all that he caught and pay his fishing account.

Now, what we made from September to December, we used to buy our food for the winter. I saw a time when we had 14 100-pound sacks of flour.

We would have a 45-gallon tierce of molasses out in the store. When we wanted a gallon of molasses, we would take out the stopper and let the molasses run out into a jug.

We had a 200-pound barrel of beef in the pantry. We had two chests of tea. Then we had two bags of hard bread for brewis during the winter.

We had thousands of potatoes. One year I remember we had 78 barrels of potatoes down in my cellar. We sold half of them. We had plenty of carrots and cabbage. We used to throw the cabbage up on the boards in our store to freeze up. We also had a full barrel of pickled cabbage. The big solid heads were cut down the middle and salted.

If you had health and strength and could work, there was no way in this world to starve a man in Bonavista. Back when I started, we were in the Depression. The whole world was in Depression. But 80% of what we ate those years, we never paid for it. We reared our own vegetables.

My father had six youngsters and he never got five cents from the government in his life. My mother always had a cooked dinner. When 'twas potatoes and turnip, we managed to get a bit of salt meat. We had our fish. The next day we had fish and brewis with potatoes and drawn butter. The next day we might have potatoes and turnip and cabbage and puddings. Then the next day we had potatoes and herring, the best kind of food.

We had molasses buns and molasses bread. My mother made up plain bread one day and the next day she made up a batch of molasses bread, because there were six children and Father and Mother. She had molasses bread with raisins and molasses buns with pork in them, all the time.

The molasses used to last us seven or eight months before it would be all gone. But it would go. Because my grandmother and my father used to sweeten their tea with molasses.

There was no one hungry, only the sick. The man who was sick, he could not work, so the government should have fed him properly. But the government was not giving him enough. Well, that man, he saw hard times. And they did see hard times, the sick.

The lazy also saw hard times. But a man that was a little bit eager, who could go fishing and come in from fishing and go in the garden and dig his ground, was okay.

Every year we had a pig. Every fall, when the cold weather came, we would kill our pig and we'd hang him up out in the store.

We kept cows for 54 years. We had thousands of milk, thousands of cream.

The women did a lot of work. They were looking after the family in the home. They helped make the fish and worked in the vegetable garden. They helped to make the hay, and tended the cattle. They kept the family going. The women in Newfoundland, they were the mainstay.

A LOT OF PEOPLE DIDN'T BELIEVE IN GHOSTS, but we did have ghosts here in Bonavista years ago.

They used to see people out around their homes, years ago, after they died. I always had a reason for that. If a man took sick, and he couldn't work, his family would go hungry. So perhaps, if he had three little children, he wouldn't be getting anything from the government. But for the crowd that lived around him, the man's family would fall on hard times.

So, if this man had tuberculosis or something like that, he got worse and worse and worse. Finally he would die.

But that man knew that after he died his children were going to be left alone in the world, with only their mother, with nobody else to provide for them.

I always used to say there was no way in the world that man could go to bed, lie down, and die with a contented mind, with three little small youngsters, knowing that they were going to be hungry. So that man, when he died, would be buried, but his spirit would always be around his family. So nighttime you could see a ghost out around that person's door. You'd meet a ghost on the street and it seemed they were always looking for something.

Now it's all in the past, because if a man got three little youngsters and a wife and if he takes sick, his youngsters would be a lot better with him gone. They're looked after more with him gone than what they would if he was home. There would be no reason why he had to worry after his death. He could die peacefully.

But years ago, people couldn't die content.

THERE'S A TREE GROWING UP in Camp Seven, what they called Camp Seven, years ago, when they used to have the sidings up there.

When the train was on, they went up to Camp Seven, about 17 miles from Bonavista. They used to put down a track so that they could push flatcars out there so that the men could load up their wood.

People had their winter camps built up there and moved their families up. There's a tree up there now between Camp Seven and Whisper Siding. Dozens of people went to that and started to chop it. You would be chopping on this side, and there be like an axe chopping on the other side of the tree. They used to have to leave it alone.

I know dozens of people who went and tried the tree and got frightened to death and they had to leave it. The tree is still there, just about chopped off. They was 'lowing that someone must have laid down by the tree and died there. He might have had a family and was worrying about them.

There are stories about ghosts wherever you go. One fella used to get on board his boat and go out into the night. When he got out on the water, there would be another fella, all dressed up for fishing, sitting out on the head of the boat. You wouldn't know but he was going out fishing with him.

I know a young girl one time who came home and looked in her living room. When she went into the room, there was a ghost sitting in the chair.

We got a ghost light out in Bonavista Bay. I've seen him hundreds of times, right out in the centre of Bonavista, halfway up to King's Cove. A girl got killed one time on a ship and they threw her over out in the middle of Bonavista Bay. Before a storm of nord'ard wind, a light appears out there in the bay.

I HAD A MAN HERE WHO TOLD ME about when he was a young man, living in Mockbeggar, here in Bonavista. In Mockbeggar there was nobody but Frenchmen buried up there. There are caskets up there sitting up on top of the ground in lots of places.

He said that he came home this night and when he got inside his gate he heard his house outside door open. And the door closed. He went in the yard. When he opened the outside door, someone opened the second door and closed it. He went in and opened the second door.

Then someone opened the kitchen door and closed it. It went on like that. When he opened the kitchen door, someone opened the hall door and went on. He heard him go up the stairs just the same as if there was a man there.

So he said, "I took off my clothes and I got something to eat. I went up the stairs. I went in my room. I got in the bed. After I got in the bed

I heard the ghost go down the stairs again. He opened the hall door and he closed it. He opened the kitchen door and he closed it. He opened the porch door and closed it and he went on out."

This happened several times when he went home, and it happened to his father before him.

"The next morning," he said, "I got up in under the house with a little rod. I pushed the rod down by every post that was keeping up the house. And here I found that one post was down and resting on top of a casket."

This is where the house had sunk down in the mud and the post settled down on the casket. He went and he got a saw, got up under the house, and sawed off that post. He took the stump that was down in the ground on the casket and took it out. He filled up the hole and he said he was never bothered with a ghost after that.

LOUISE (EMBERLEY) HOLLETT

Tidal Wave: On Great Burin Island

Louise Hollett is a senior citizen living in Burin Bay. She was 23 years old when the tidal wave hit her town of Great Burin on Great Burin Island. Louise was in the kitchen enjoying the smells from the oven when she heard a noise.

"I WAS IN THE HOUSE," Mrs. Hollett recalls. "It was about 5:00. We were getting supper. We had a lady come over to visit us that day and Mom was baking apple dumplings. That's what she had in the oven, apple dumplings.

"I don't know what else we were going to have, but I know we were going to have these, maybe for dessert or something. I heard this noise and I thought it was the stove. We ran out by the door and you could feel the earth shaking under your feet."

To the Telegraph Office

After supper, Louise made her way to the telegraph office. Up and away from the beach there was a road called the "high road," but she took the route down by the water. Parts of the lower walkway were simply planks laid across fish flakes, joined by bridges. The harbour was to her left as she walked.

"I went over to hear the news, and when I was going over, the harbour went right dry. Darby's boat was there and she was high and dry at the wharf.

"In the post office they used to have telegraphy. Mrs. Helen Darby was the telegraph operator and she had a big news book. The news would come and she would write it all out and then put it out in the lobby. Sometimes she would read it for the crowd of men standing around.

"After the earthquake, they came over from Shalloway," recalls Mrs. Hollett. "That's another island they had to come over footbridges to get there. They came over to hear the news and see what was happening."

THE TIDAL WAVE

"I WASN'T OVER THERE VERY LONG, only a few minutes, when I heard the big rush, and the water all rushed in."

Luckily, the water did not come up to where Louise was standing. "The telegraph office was up higher. There were the wharves and then you came up a little bit to what they called the beach. They had beaches down there where they used to make fish. Then there was an upgrade to the telegraph office.

"Everybody went up on higher ground. And we were scared stiff. The funny thing was, we didn't know what a tidal wave was. We were quite ignorant of what was happening. We thought the place was sinking or something.

"There was a lighthouse keeper up there, from somewhere in England. Sidney Hussey was his name. He told us what was happening. 'You know, when there's an earthquake, there is usually a tidal wave if it is out in the ocean.'"

Seeing the damage on the beach, the visitors from Shalloway became nervous. They had good reason to be uneasy. "The Shalloway people lived right down on beaches," says Mrs. Hollett.

"They thought their houses would be gone. They got the ferry boat that was there and tried to go over to see how their families were and see what was gone. Do you know, they couldn't steer the thing at all, with so much tide. They finally got there, and there was hardly a thing damaged."

WORRIED ABOUT MOTHER

AT THE TELEGRAPH OFFICE, LOUISE WAS WORRIED. "I was out by the door, looking and listening. Everybody was looking. I didn't know what to do. My mother was home and we lived down near the water. I went home by way of the high road and called out to her. She and this other woman came up over the hill."

On the slope, the whole community gathered to watch. "Mr. E. M. Hollett had a store where he used to keep lumber and other things. You could hear all the lumber tumbling out of his store, as the high tide took all his wharves out to sea. Some of the lumber lodged on the bank and in the landwash. All night long we could hear the men trying to salvage it and throw it up on high land."

Great Burin did not sustain as much damage as other villages on Great Burin Island. "It came in there and went down through the Reach and down in Stepaside, but in Kelly's Cove it got pinned there. It brought up there, so they had more damage than the rest. Then it went on down to Port au Bras. It sort of passed along by us."

A Night Away from Home

"BELIEVE IT OR NOT, the magistrate lived in Great Burin. He was Malcolm Hollett. He served in the First World War, and after the war he was honoured as a Rhodes Scholar and went to England and received his degrees. When he came back he became a magistrate and later served in the Newfoundland government.

"He was instrumental in helping organize provisions and help for those affected by the tidal wave. He was my mother's first cousin and it was to his house we went and stayed when the tidal wave was at its worst."

Father Arrives

TWO OR THREE DAYS AFTER THE TIDAL WAVE, Louise's father sailed into Great Burin.

"My father was Joseph Emberley. He and another man went down to Swift Current cutting wood, because hardly anybody lived there then. The other man had one of these little jack boats. They ran up in the bottom, which they call Piper's Hole.

"That evening, they noticed that the tide was pretty high, and swirling. The boat used to spin around, but he didn't know what was causing it. He didn't know anything about what was happening. But when they were coming home they met the wreckage of things and found out it was the tidal wave."

BERKLEY INGRAM

RECOLLECTIONS OF PLACENTIA BAY

Berkley Ingram lives in the Golden Years Manor at Arnold's Cove. Except for a few years in St. John's, he lived all his life in Placentia Bay.

I WAS BORN JANUARY 17, 1912, at Woody Island, Placentia Bay. I went to school a short while at Woody Island. At only seven years old I helped my mother trench potatoes.

I remember one very stormy day. It was snowing and cold, but not windy. My father and another man had to go approximately three miles over ice, towing a sleigh to get a lady, a Mrs. Bollard who was a midwife.

They had to wrap the lady in blankets in the sleigh. Then, with ropes over their shoulders, they towed Mrs. Bollard and the sleigh all the way from Bollard's Point to our house on Allen's Point.

I cannot remember much more about Woody Island, as I was not eight years old when I left home. My cousin and his wife came to visit Mother, who was his aunt. They had no children and they asked Mom and Dad if they would let me go with them. Mom and Dad talked it over and decided that I could go. They knew I would be well cared for.

My cousin's wife was, I always said, an angel. I was given the best of everything and treated like a prince. Walter Ingram, the cousin who adopted me, was a teacher before taking the job as telegraph operator and postmaster. I learned telegraphy at age 10 while helping him by delivering messages around and sorting the mail. I had to be sworn in to use the telegraph at age 12.

About a year after, we encountered line trouble for three or four days. We had to get a boat and take whatever messages were on hand to Argentia to be transmitted to St. John's. En route, a fire started in the engine room. There were two 45-gallon tanks of gas, one on each side of the engine room. We were lucky to have salt in the hold of the boat, and that is what the engineer threw on the fire to extinguish it.

Another time my cousin, his wife, and I left Tacks Beach to go to Harbour Buffett in open boat. On the way, something happened which caused a fire around the engine room. The man attending the engine drew water from the dill room, which only increased the fire. Then he had to draw water over the side of the boat to extinguish it.

At age 14 I went to work with the firm of Alberto Wareham & Sons as sales clerk in their general store. When not busy there, I went down to the fish store to help pack the dry codfish. Four hundred and forty-eight pounds of fish were put in each cask and pressed down with a heavy screw by two men. That fish was exported to Spain, Denmark, Portugal, and Barbados.

After working with Warehams' for a couple of years, I went to St. John's. I opened a confectionery store on Boncloddy Street. After a year I moved down to New Gower Street. I was only there about a year when the Shop Act came in. Then I had to screen off the grocery side with wire netting, and was only allowed to sell confectionery after 6:00 p.m.

I went to work with Alberto Wareham & Sons again. Before Newfoundland joined Confederation, when supplies were brought in by their boats from PEI or other foreign places, they would put a tide-waiter on board to enforce customs regulations.

One of their boats came from PEI with produce for their firm at Spencer's Cove. After the cargo was unloaded, the boat was light in ballast. We left Spencer's Cove to return to Harbour Buffett and the wind was very strong. Coming around Buffett headland, one gust of wind in the sails caused the boat to lean over enough that the tip of the sail's boom touched the sea.

Here is another memory. One winter I fell on an axe and cut a piece of flesh completely out of my leg. After about a week, proud flesh came in the cut. Someone got clamshells, crushed them to a powder, and sprinkled it on the cut and it healed in a short time. I have the scar on my leg for anyone to see now, at age 86.

JAMES JOHN

"Just There" Was a Long Way

James John is an expert Gander River guide living in Glenwood, Newfoundland. With his native heritage, he has a special feeling for the land and water around him. He learned his guiding skills from his father, James John Sr.

FATHER'S STYLE WAS TO catch or kill only what you could eat, what you're going to supply for the winter. Even when we had to go and kill caribou to eat ourselves, we were only allowed one. One caribou could do us a month. After that month was over, he would send us up for another one.

He'd only give us two bullets each, me and my brother. I was 18 or 19 then, and right accurate, longing for the time to come. But he would hold off and send us up in the right time of the year, in July or August, to make the kill.

We would go up to Northwest Gander, up on our trapping ground. We would spend four or five days, or a week up there, hunting, because caribou weren't plentiful then. You had to wait for them a lot.

We would sit and wait until the right time, when we could hear them way off in the distance. Whenever there were four or five caribou together, we could hear the noise from their hooves.

You waited when it was calm, or when the wind was blowing your way. You waited until you knew they were coming your way. Then you went towards them to get handier and handier to the noise. By and by, sure enough, you'd see them and you'd pick out one of the caribou.

It had to be a boren doe (barren doe), Dad used to call it, a caribou that never had no calf. He wouldn't kill either one that had a calf, or a stag. My dad used to tell us how they used to tell them apart. Those Indians, like Dad, grew up in the woods, so they knew exactly what they were looking for.

A boren doe had the best meat. We had to be able to tell a boren doe from another doe or a stag. Well, you could tell a stag, because he probably had little bunches on his head, horns. A doe who had a calf had a long tail, eight or nine inches.

But the boren doe had a little short tail, because it never had any calf. It's so fat around the rump, it fills out the tail, so that it looks like they only got a short one. This is how you tell them apart.

My father was a big man. He was six foot two. He could carry a lot of meat on his back. I have seen him put a full caribou on his back, a caribou with just the guts cut out of it. He tied two legs together and hauled it down over his back. With his rifle under his arm, we had to go 15 miles, and he never put that caribou down!

Once I was carrying the liver, heart, and the kidneys, in a little packsack. Every half an hour I said, "Dad, when are you going to stop? How far have we got to go?"

He said, "Just there." He wouldn't say how far, in miles. "Just there."

That "just there" was a long ways.

C. MILLEY JOHNSON

MAURA FALTON

C. Milley Johnson is an active senior in the Little Catalina–Port Union area. "Maura Falton" was a valentine greeting common in areas of Newfoundland settled by people from England. It is from the expression Good Morrow Valentine. It was shortened to Morrow Valentine, and with an outport dialect became "Maura Falton."

I RACED ACROSS THE GARDEN as fast as the devil could scorch a feather. It was February 14, and I wanted to "Maura Falton" Uncle George before anyone else was up. Whoever Maura Faltoned him first would get 50 cents, and that was a lot of money 50 years ago.

Aunt Sue was up cleaning the old Waterloo before she lit the fire and the stove would get too hot. It was freezing indoors as well as out, but I didn't mind that. I sat on the chair nearest the hall door.

Aunt Sue had an old wool sock hauled over her hand for the final touch to the stove. I couldn't see how she could make it shine more than it already did, but she gave it a brisk once-over, then neatly folded the sock, put it in the blackening box, and stored it under the stairs.

She was smiling to herself and looked like I imagined Mrs. Santa Claus looked. She had a frilly dust cap on and a big apron that covered her entire dress, and a black spot on the side of her cheek.

Her eyes twinkled despite her age. She was the best "old aunt" in the community. She gave the children more "martrimonies"—small raisin tarts—than all the other women who lived there. Without saying a word, she went to the sideboard and produced one for me as if by magic, and then, laying the kindling in the stove, it wasn't long before the pleasant crackle of burning wood could be heard.

The two rungs in the front of the chair I sat on were missing and I could swing my legs in and out as fast as I wanted. I was calculating in my head what I would buy at Uncle Will's shop with my 50 cents.

Five Union Squares—they were my favourite—soft marshmallow squares, pink and white and covered with sugar. Oh yes, I can get those delicious licorice—10 of these I can afford—and ring sticks. I'd have as many rings as Selina, who had one on nearly all her fingers because her father owned the store. I could also afford a few chocolate mice for Nanna, who never grew up when it came to eating candy, especially chocolate mice. That must be who I inherited my sweet tooth from. No common candy for me today. That was okay when you only had a cent.

The outside door rattled and my heart ceased to beat. Was Neddy coming too? Neddy was my cousin from up the road. But I didn't hear another sound, only a chair being moved upstairs. Oh, the agony! Wouldn't Uncle George ever come down?

I was imagining Uncle George kneeling by the bed saying his prayers, because everything had gone quiet upstairs. I spoke for the first time. "Aunt Sue, do you think Uncle George is getting up?"

"Yes, me maid, he'll be down in a minute. 'Tis cold up there and that's the thing he don't like since he got old."

Then there was a sound like thunder. I nearly jumped out of my skin. "He's killed, Aunt Sue!"

She didn't move. She just looked at me and laughed. "Das the rock he keeps in the bed to keep it warm. Seems he dropped it."

I "scrouged" around on the chair until the seat must be gone out of my pants, my legs swinging faster than the pendulum on the clock.

I felt like running upstairs, but one would never do that, so I just sat there praying silently that Neddy wouldn't get there before Uncle George got downstairs.

I heard the porch door open and I said to myself, "That's it. The little devil is here. Now I'll have to share my money." I had never been lucky enough to get it because Neddy was "bolder" than I was, and he'd open the hall door and call out, but I could not do that, chicken that I was.

The door opened and there was Aunt Ad. "Suse, can I have the loan of your broom to sweep up? Mine came all abroad last night."

Oh, what a relief. I couldn't stand Aunt Ad. Nanna always said she was a "maw-mouth," but I was sure glad to see her now, instead of Neddy.

Then I heard the plump, squeak, plump, squeak, coming down the stairs and I started to swing my legs faster and faster. "Faura Malton" went through my mind. Oh no, that's not right!

"Keep your head on straight, girl," I could hear Nanna say.

The door opened and I was struck dumb. Not a word would come. I heard the porch door close or open, I didn't know which, and then it came to mind. "Maura Falton, Uncle George!"

He stood by the stove, rubbing his hands together, ignoring me. I'm going to die if he doesn't do something, I thought. Maybe I didn't say it. Should I try again? Then he turned and looked at me and the loveliest smile I have ever seen on a person's face in my life greeted me. "Well, Kari maid, you beat Neddy after all."

He put his hand in his pocket, rattled some change, and came up with the shiniest half-dollar you ever saw. He passed it to me and I put my arms around his neck and kissed him over and over.

"Ah, Kari my dear, you are a real kisser. God bless you." Tears came in his eyes and I knew he was remembering his own granddaughter who was living in Toronto, whom he only got to see in the summer.

I don't know what "Maura Falton" means even to this day, but it was always the custom that whoever Maura Faltoned you first on St. Valentine's Day, you had to give them a gift. Uncle George was my favourite because he always gave 50 cents.

GORDON LANNON

TRAIN CONDUCTOR

Gordon Lannon lives in Bishop's Falls. He joined the Newfoundland railway in 1944 and retired in 1985. His father was working for the railway when Gordon was hired.

AFTER I GOT MY DISCHARGE from the army, in 1944, I got a job with the railway. I wanted to be a locomotive engineer. Well, I was going to go firing at first. You started as a fireman, shovelling coal.

We lived in Kilbride at the time. When I was a boy, the trains used to go up through Bowring Park. The locomotive would be pulling the train up the hill. I'd see them when the fireman shovelled the coal in, in the nighttime. She would be going up the grade, and you would see the black smoke coming out of the stack, into the sky.

So anyway, I went out and I applied for a job with the railway. You had to go as a student fireman at that time. I saw the chief engineer. He said, "Well, we'll give you an opportunity, a chance to prove yourself."

I went home and I told Dad. Now, he was the type of man, when he said no, he meant no. We were sitting down to supper. I forget how many were at the table, but there were quite a few of us there.

He said, "No, you're not going on any locomotive, because I don't want you to end up like a few other poor unfortunates that were killed on the railway."

Charlie Cahill had been killed out at Northern Bight shortly before that. The locomotive went off the track and turned over and they couldn't get out, and they were scalded.

I said, "Very good." I wouldn't go against him for all the tea in China.

So I left the next day and I told the superintendent, "Dad doesn't want me to go firing on the locomotive."

He said, "What about a job braking?"

I said, "Fine, anything at all."

He looked over his glasses at me across his desk. He said, "Why would you want to go to work with the railway?"

"Well sir, I'm tired of living off my father. I'd like to go on my own."

That was the fourth of December [1944]. The next morning they sent me up to see Dr. O'Regan on Patrick Street. He gave me a medical and sent me back. Mr. W.J. Chafe used to be chief inspector. He and Leo Brazil were in the dispatching office, so he sent me out to get a rule book and a switch key.

I went home. Dad wasn't there, and I told Mom, "I got a job with the railway."

The next morning, about 6:30 a.m., the phone rang and this was the dispatcher. He said, "If you want to, you can go to Argentia."

It was a mixed train. We had a baggage car, a mail car, and a couple of coaches. We'd pick up passengers along the way at Whitbourne, going to Argentia.

Anyway, we went to Argentia and we came back. I made several more runs after that with the same crew. A couple of days later I was called to go to Bishop's Falls on a freight train. At that time they were moving paper from Grand Falls to St. John's, because Botwood was icebound. Anyway, we left St. John's with 13 cars.

We came to Clarenville. When I got off there, here was Dad coming down the stand. That was about 3:00 in the afternoon. He looked, and I don't think he could believe his eyes. "What are you doing here?"

I said, "I got a job braking."

He shook his head and he laughed. He said, "You were bound to get a job with the railway, to go railroading, weren't you?"

MADELINE LANNON

CAUGHT IN THE ACT!

Madeline Lannon of Grand Falls can tell many stories about her life as a registered nurse. During World War II she was nursing in Argentia. Some mornings Madeline and her roommate entertained the sailors, without knowing it.

THE LARGE LIVING ROOM windows in the nurses' residence opened out French-style. It was July month, in 1942, at Argentia, Newfoundland. Every morning when Blanche Dunphy and I came off night duty, we used to watch the sailors on the USS *Prairie* do their PT exercises.

The *Prairie* was moored at the wharf, just down from the residence. Blanche and I decided that we would do the exercises along with the sailors. We would open the French windows, strip down to our bra and panties, and do the exercises. Blanche and I never felt so smug, or self-satisfied.

We felt so good afterwards, until one night, when my world fell apart. I was at work, nursing a sailor off the *Prairie*. He told me what fun he and his buddies had, watching two girls at the nurses' residence do their exercises. They used to take turns with binoculars.

It's a wonder I didn't explode. We never realized we were putting on a free show for Uncle Sam's boys!

PT: physical training

HOWARD LETHBRIDGE

Trapper from Paradise River

Howard Lethbridge lived the hard life of a fur trapper. It was a beautiful, sunny day when I visited him in Cartwright, Labrador. It was late in August, but already you could feel that the fall weather was very near. It would soon be winter, the best time to trap for fur.

MY FATHER, PHILLIP LETHBRIDGE, trapped for 40 years. I learned from my father. Of course, I started off very young. I wasn't quite 10 years old the first time I made a short trip in the country. That trip was about two nights long, in November. It was cold then, with quite a lot of ice. There wasn't much snow but there was quite a lot of ice around. The frost comes in November down here, sometimes in October.

Father had his trapping line in from Paradise River, where we lived. We started right from the house. In a day, we walked four miles to our first cabin.

I was just a little over 14 when I took off on my own, trapping. I trapped on my father's trap ground. He was just about giving it up. I did a lot of trapping alone, but some years I had a buddy, or perhaps one of my brothers.

THE TRAPLINE

WE HAD OUR FIRST TRAP a half-hour walk from home. That's where we'd start setting traps, and we continued on up our trapline, with traps so far apart.

Around four hours was the average walk to where the cabin was. That's as much as you could make in a short day in the winter when tending your traps, setting your traps, and resetting.

We didn't start trapping until around the middle of October. That was when the season was open, and we'd trap until the first part of April, most of the time. After that, furs weren't much good because they would be shedding.

Where I would end up trapping, it would be 70 and 80 miles to walk. It was not that far, walking in a straight line. But you would crook around a lot and go in different directions. The nearest mountains where I would turn back was the Hawk's Mountain.

The average trip would be four or five weeks, but some trips were seven and eight. About eight weeks was the longest I was trapping, away from home for a long time.

CABINS AND TENTS

WE ONLY HAD TWO CABINS on the fall trapping ground, we called it. When the wintertime came, when we could haul all our luggage, we'd have a canvas tent. We'd haul our tent and stove and all our food on a sled. We wouldn't have any cabins in the winter at all, but set up our camp every night.

We had a little stove about two feet long, and eight or nine inches square. We'd have plenty of heat with that set up in the middle of the tent.

In bad weather you'd spread your fly over the ridgepole. That would keep your camp from getting wet, when it was snowing. If you didn't have that, sometimes you'd have a lot of leaking, where the snow melted directly on your tent.

We used to haul a little sled and we sometimes had a couple of dogs pulling a small komatik.

If you killed caribou to haul home, perhaps you'd have four to six dogs. You would have quite a large komatik then, of course, loaded up with caribou.

I guess I was trapping around 25 years. After a while I got kind of crippled up. I wasn't so good at it, so I had to give it up. You had to be quite tough to trap like that.

THERE USED TO BE A LOT OF WOLVES some years when I was trapping, but they were hard to see. They kept away from us all the time. Except for the two that I saw when I had no gun one time.

I went to check my traps one morning and there was a lot of snow. To reset the trap I had to dig it out of six feet of snow, down to the water. I got down there and reset my trap and when I came up I looked out on the brook. There were two wolves coming towards me.

They were showing their teeth, kind of half scared, I suppose, and growling. All I had was my axe and my iron shovel. I didn't know what they were going to do, attack me or not. I started banging on my old iron shovel with the axe and shouted at the same time. That kind of scared them.

One turned around and went back on his trail where he was coming. The other one just circled out around me a little ways and took my snowshoe track back in the direction of my cabin where I came from. That was the last I saw of them.

FLORENCE MacDONALD

CAMPBELL'S CREEK IN THE '40S AND '50S

Florence MacDonald and her husband, Mike, wrested a good living from the sea and off the land. From early morning to late night, Mrs. MacDonald worked hard to raise her family, keep a good home, and help in the gardens. It was a hard but healthy life.

I WAS BORN IN BOSWARLOS in 1919. Florence Janes. I married Mike MacDonald from Campbell's Creek. His sister and her husband—a fisherman—had a nice-sized little farm and I used to work there. He used to come and visit his sister, and that's how come I met up with him.

They had six milch cows. It was hard work to milk six cows morning and evening, and do housework too. I fed the calves and the pigs. There was a lot of outdoor work to be done.

They made their own hay. I helped at turning the hay over, and then helped in the house. There was a lot of hard work. You worked hard them days for $5 a month.

Those days, when they were 20 or 25 years of age, young people built their own homes. Mike lived with his brother and his mother, so I suppose he figured some day he would move out and get married.

He had the house built 10 years. It wasn't quite finished, but it was livable. It was good enough to live in. To build your house, you only needed the nails and your felt, because you cut all your own wood and got it sawed. You had everything, except glass and lime. It had wood shingles on it, and it wasn't painted for a long time.

MARRIED LIFE

MY HUSBAND, MIKE, WAS A FISHERMAN out of Campbell's Creek. He was older than I was. He died about 15 years ago. He was 83.

He fished here, and we had a farm too. We owned all the land from here, way up to another field back there, and we kept cattle, sheep and cows. We had two cows, some sheep, and a horse for hauling the wood and ploughing the land.

We had two milch cows and we'd have their calves. We kept them over a winter and we'd kill them the next fall for our beef. We lived good. We didn't go to the store for too much, only for sugar, flour, and tea.

In the fall we'd have one or two pigs to kill, and chickens. We would kill about 30 or 40 chickens, and we'd keep about 10 or 12 for over winter. We had our own eggs and our fresh butter, we called it then, homemade butter.

To make butter, you had to have a separator to separate the cream from the milk. You saved up the cream, and then you used a churn. There were all kinds of churns. Some had a dasher churn and some others had churns that spun around, with a crank in them. You could make it by hand, too, with a spoon in a pan.

We had no fridges, but we had a nice cold spring of water. We could put the cream in that overnight to cool it in the hot summertime. I used to sell a nice bit of butter. Thirty cents a pound, I used to get for butter. Sometimes I would sell 10 pounds a week. It was a lot of money, and that could help to buy the things that we couldn't grow.

We had our own vegetables. The only things we got from a merchant were flour and tea, sugar and molasses, and salt.

You could salt your own beef if you had your own cattle. You'd have a pig to kill and you'd have a yearling to kill and maybe one to sell. The cows would have their calves in the spring. You'd always keep two over winter. By the next fall they were a nice size. They would be 200 and 300 pounds by the second fall. That way you always had something to kill for fresh beef and to make salt beef. We also had to bottle some because there were no freezers or no fridges then. You'd have to bottle it if you wanted it fresh, but when the cold weather was on, starting in November, your meat would be frozen until the spring, until April anyway.

My husband used to catch lobster, starting in April, and he fished salmon and a bit of codfish. There wasn't much price for anything then, but you had lots for yourself to eat. Then, around the last part of December, he would go at the smelt fishing, out at Piccadilly.

There was a big basin, and they would set nets there. When the harbour froze over, they would set nets through the ice, under the ice. He used to get 10 cents a pound for them, not very much.

This was in the '30s and '40s. They had to ship that away to Boston to get 10 cents a pound. It was frozen. They had some kind of a cold place out to Piccadilly. Well, the winters were so cold then, you used to freeze them yourself. You'd spread them out and freeze them and pack them in boxes and they shipped them away.

In the summer, I would spread the fish for my husband, that's all. I was kept pretty busy in the house. We had 11 children! I had quite a busy day.

The cows were milked twice a day. You'd be out 8:00 or earlier to milk them. There was no radio or TV, and when it got dark you couldn't work out of doors. You only had the lamplight in the wintertime. I used to have to card my wool to knit the mitts and socks and sweaters and then I would spin the yarn in the nighttime. I never had much time in the day. It would take you pretty well the best part of your day to do washes, by the time you carried your water and you heated it on the stove and washed in a tub, using a scrub board. Well, you would have most of the day gone by then.

I would have to mix and bake nearly every day. They liked a lot of bread and molasses. Their father liked to have molasses on his bread and they all followed—molasses bread.

The children would pick the raspberries and partridgeberries and blueberries. They were the main ones. Bakeapples were farther away. A few places, way back on the hills, we'd get a gallon or so, but at

Shoal Point, now, that's where the bakeapples grew, way out there. The children were good. They all kept busy. They all did their work. It's not like today. It's sad today. Children don't know how to do anything like that today.

We had three bedrooms and in the living room we would have a daybed that pulled out. Then according's they got older, 18 and 19, they got out on their own.

But they keep coming back. They love to come back home. I kept some of them when they first got married, until they got out on their own. But they all got their own homes now. They're doing all right. I have six great-grandchildren.

WASH DAY

NOBODY WORKED ON SUNDAY. Except, you had to milk the cows. You'd rest up on Sunday a bit, except for meals and that.

Wash day, you just got up in the morning and carried your water from this little spring. It took an hour or so to get that all heated up and poured into your tub. As soon as you got that in your tub, you'd start scrubbing on the board.

We had the Waterloo stove. It was a flat wood stove with a round oven on it.

The Waterloo was blocked with boilers. There wouldn't be any dinner cooked that day. After the pots were off, we could cook our supper. Supper, we called it then. They call it dinner now.

We'd cook dinner on Sunday, and the pot liquor off your Sunday dinner, you'd save it. On Monday you'd make soup with it, probably for dinner. That was only easy to make. Tuesday we'd have meat again and Wednesday we would have fish.

On Thursday it was a meat day and on Friday was fish again. Saturday would be just something light, maybe make up hash or have some little stew or something. On Sunday we'd have the big dinner.

You'd have something light for supper on Mondays and Saturdays. Perhaps you'd have stew, in different ways.

It wasn't until the early 1950s when I got this stove with the fancy water tank on it. We did very good that summer. And I had a gasoline washer that same time. Until then I used the scrub board and washtub.

We had the bare, white lumber floor at first. You had to get down on your hands and knees and scrub that with a brush once a week. That was hard to keep clean with a crowd of kids.

We also got a floor covering for the kitchen floor. We used to call it mill canvas. It was white, heavy stuff, and we painted that. When we got this mill canvas, we painted it a nice brown. It was pretty good too.

My husband never made any big money, but nobody went hungry. Things weren't good for people who didn't have a husband.

We used to eat a nice lot of potatoes. For sure we used 30 pounds a week, or maybe more. We also had parsnip and other vegetables. Our cellar was under the house.

We bottled jams, we bottled meat, and if we got any rabbit worthwhile, we'd bottle rabbit, and different things.

Sometimes we would bury turnip and cabbage. They kept good there, below the frost, and coming on the spring, we'd dig them out.

A lot of people had outside cellars dug in the side of a hill. We never used to have much for all year around, though. We would have ours pretty well eaten up by the spring, or the early part of the summer.

SHEEP

WE NEVER HAD TOO MUCH LUCK WITH SHEEP, seven or eight, that's all. They would find lambs in the spring, and we would kill them in the fall. That was a good treat then.

We had the wool for knitting socks and mitts, and caps and sweaters.

The wool was washed then, scalded. You'd rig up boilers outside to scald your wool and then you had to pick that wool. Here in Campbell's Creek, we would go from house to house for what they called a picking spree. A crowd would come to my house one evening after supper and they'd all pick my wool. I'd make a lunch. Then probably a few nights later, we went to someone else's place. We had a nice lot of wool. In the first few years we didn't send it away. We could card it ourselves to make our rolls, and we would spin them.

Later we found a place where we could send it away and get the rolls made. In the latter years we found out we could send it out to Prince Edward Island and get blankets made. Oh, we got beautiful blankets from there, made out of the wool. And it didn't cost too much to get that done.

There's no one who keeps sheep any more around here.

I used to knit underwear, long johns, bottom and top. I used to knit it in two pieces. You had to knit underwear because when they were smelt fishing on the ice it would be terrible cold. The winters were cold then and they would have to be out on that ice all day long, so they would have to have the woollen underwear. Let me tell you, I did some knitting.

You'd have to have a shift, two lots. I don't know how I did it, to tell the truth.

People still tell me they find the days long, but I never saw a day since I've been born that I found it a long day. I keep busy all the time, all the time. You get into that and you can't stop.

MAKING CLOTHES

I'LL TELL YOU NOW WHERE I USED TO GET MY CLOTHES. People that I knew, they were well-to-do, they would give me clothes. I had people, friends and relatives far away, and they would send me parcels. They would send me coats, real expensive mink coats, and seal coats, and all those kinds of things. I would cut them down and make coats for my smaller children.

They never went out much in the cold when they were small. They had a sweater on, and a coat. You could buy a bit of material. It wasn't too expensive then. Windbreaker material, you'd call it, for coats.

We used flour sacks for sheets. You would bleach them and make them nice and sew them. That would be for sheets and pillowcases. Some of the flour sacks were dyed black, to make pants for the children. The children would wear knitted underwear underneath the black pants.

In the woods you could pick a certain kind of moss off a tree, a spruce tree. That would make a brown dye. It would stay. It was used for their socks. You even knit the girls' socks, right to the knee. You had to knit all year round to get caught up on it, to have something for everyone to wear.

My goodness, I knit hundreds of vamps. And mitts. The men in the woods would wear out a lot of mitts, and when fishing too.

FISHING WAS HARD

WHEN MY HUSBAND STARTED FISHING first, he fished with a man called Danny. Daniel Campbell. He was 16 when he first went fishing. There wasn't much work then. That would have been in 1916.

There were no motors. After they hauled their lobster pots, they would row them in to Abbott and Haliburton. They had to row all the way along the shore from here to there in those days. All that, and they only got a cent and a half a pound for their lobster. If the wind came up too rough, they had to stay there until the wind calmed down.

Then the two of them would row the boat back. 'Twas hard work. The pay they got for all that work wasn't very much.

Down here it's a real hard place for a fisherman.

HOMEMADE BLEACH

THEY USE JAVEX NOW FOR BLEACHING. We used to have a big iron boiler on the stove and we used lye, little flakes of powerful stuff. Shake some of that in your water and you would scald your clothes. You would wash in it, and scald it, and rinse it.

If we didn't have any of this canned lye, we used to save our wood ashes from the wood stove. We would put the ashes into a boiler and steep it on the stove, and then we would take it off to cool. That's just as good as the canned lye. It'd be right clear.

HOMEMADE SOAP

WHEN YOU KILLED YOUR ANIMALS in the fall they would have a lot of fat on them. You'd trim all that off and save it. You'd boil that on the stove and put this canned lye into it. After it boiled for so long, there would be nothing left. The fat would be all boiled out. We dipped out any lumps and let the rest set in the pot. Then we'd cut it out in junks and put it away. It would dry right hard to make beautiful soap.

We used to use only the animal fat, but now, a lot of people, like Father and others, they also made it from a little seal fat. It had a terrible smell. And there's fat in the cod oil. We used to make soap out of that, but it was terrible. You'd rinse the clothes a lot, but the smell wouldn't come off.

But the fat from your meats didn't smell so bad.

GARDENS

WE PUT IN POTATOES, turnip, cabbage, beets and carrot, parsnips and grew pumpkins and zucchinis. I grew some very big pumpkins. Not that long ago, I think it was '88, I planted my garden, and then I went to Ontario. When I came back it was still July and there were only four plants. The rest didn't come.

By the last part of September I had four large pumpkins. I had a

45-pound one, a 50, a 55, and a 60. They were the biggest ones I ever grew. The rest of the time I only had small ones. Ten or 15 pounds would be the biggest.

We would grow cucumbers and cauliflower too and make up our own pickles. Bread and butter pickles, and mustard pickles. We'd make a nice bit of that. After we got a deep freeze, we would boil down our turnip tops. We grew our own onions too, you know.

My husband would plow the land. We used the horse in the garden. He would be busy at the fishing, but he would help me to make the drills. I would have to do the planting, and as soon as the children were big enough, at six or seven, they would help to drop the potato seed.

Both of us did the weeding. That was the killer, when the weeds got out of hand. In the gardens we used stable manure, sheep manure. We also used herring. We set our potato seeds so that they were a herring-length apart. Later years we could buy fertilizer.

We would dig the potatoes, dry them, and put them in bags and put them in the cellar for the winter. My husband did the lifting. After the potatoes were in the cellar, he would be cutting wood for the winter. When the snow came, he would haul the wood out with the horse.

We wouldn't have enough wood to do us all year round, because we had to keep our fire on for heating the pots of water, every day.

THE VINEGAR PLANT

WE USED TO HAVE OUR OWN VINEGAR, too. We'd have our own vinegar plant growing in a bottle of water. The plant is a vellum, almost like a jellyfish. You add sugar and the plant turns it into vinegar.

HOME REMEDIES

YOU COULD MAKE YOUR OWN COUGH MEDICINE out of white spruce. You took the bark off the tree and inside that was kind of a white vellum. You boiled that on the stove. You put a bit of sugar with it and made your own cough medicine. I haven't made any for a long time now. I used to put something else in it, a bit of vinegar and sugar. Probably molasses. That would stop your cough a bit, especially if you had a real bad one.

You never heard tell of turkey much for Christmas. You would have a goose. You'd save that goose grease and you'd rub that on the children's chests and on their backs. You'd give them cod oil to drink for their cold.

You'd give the children cod oil all the time. A teaspoon in the morning. Some of them liked it, more of them didn't. One of my children, I'm not sure which one it was, loved it! I had to keep the bottle hidden from her. There were some more then who weren't too happy about having to take it.

MIDWIVES WEREN'T NECESSARY

I HAD A DOCTOR ATTEND TO ME for most of my babies. The midwife would come with the doctor. I only had to go to the hospital twice. You only went then if it was an emergency.

Sarah March was a midwife. She died a long time ago. She was a relative of mine. After she was gone, my sister-in-law used to come in. Her name was Sarah MacDonald. She died a nice while back, too. Then there used to be another woman by the name of Mrs. Millie Campbell. She was here one time.

A lot used to say babies came from in under a stump. You also heard the doctor dropped them. I guess I was 10 or 12 years old before we figured that the doctor must have dropped them. Not today!

They'd say, if you were pregnant, you couldn't reach up to touch anything. Some would say if you saw food and if you liked to have that food, wherever you put your hand there would be a birthmark. You were wishing probably you'd have a certain kind of berry or some kind of meat, and if you put your hand on your face or your arms or wherever, there would be a birthmark left on the new baby.

I know children born with birthmarks, all right, but I don't know for sure if it was from that or not. I know a relative of mine, she was about seven months pregnant. She was driving in the car with her husband, and she thought there was going to be an accident. She put her hands over her face, and when her child was born, over half his face was a different colour.

CHARMERS AND REMEDIES

IF YOU HAD A BAD TOOTHACHE? There was one person, a seventh son, who lived next door. He was what you would call a charmer. If anyone got a bad toothache or a bad pain, they would take their child to him and he would make the sign of the cross and say a little prayer. He died young with cancer.

There was a cure older people had for people who had asthma bad, like children. They would cut a lock off their hair, bore a hole in a tree, and put it in there. They'd just leave it there, I suppose, and after so long the asthma would go away.

If you had a bad earache, some would slice an onion and put that over your ear. Some more would mix up mustard and flour to make a poultice. The poultice was put in a cloth and wrapped around your head to lodge it against your ear.

Some others would get a salt herring, if they had a real bad sore throat. They'd wrap it in a little cloth and tie it around the throat. I never tried it myself. My husband tried it. He said it worked. His sore throat went away.

Three children in my husband's family died of diphtheria, in one week. He was the baby of the family. The doctor used to come and give them something he called the "kill or cure." When he'd come back the next day they would be dead. Three died like that.

In those days, the grandmother was the boss in the house. When couples married, the grandmothers lived in. When children came, there would be three generations in one house at the same time.

They told my husband, Mike, this story when he got older. This time, the old grandmother was there when the doctor came. The doctor was going to give him the "kill or cure."

The grandmother grabbed the doctor and pushed him right out the door!

She said, "You've killed enough now. You get out!"

That was a long time ago. That was in 1900.

JACK MAY

TWILLINGATE LIGHTHOUSE KEEPER

Jack May of Twillingate carries on the old tradition of lighthouse keepers. I met him at the lighthouse and he told me a little of its history.

THE HISTORY OF THE LIGHTHOUSE, if it was written, I never saw it. And I could never get any information out of Jack Roberts, God rest his soul. He died two falls ago, I guess it was, at the age of 96 or 98. He would never talk about his work at Long Point.

His father was Robert Samuel Roberts. Of course that was shortened to Bob Sam. He was the first principal lightkeeper here. As far as we know, he started here, in 1876, with a lightkeeper by the name of Henry Preston, who came over from England. Now, Henry Preston, it is generally surmised, and I guess mostly by me, was probably an expert on the mechanisms for lighthouses.

He came over as an expert and worked with Bob Sam Roberts, and they were both here together. He stayed in Newfoundland. As a matter of fact, he died and is buried in the United Church Cemetery on the north side.

Except for the tower, there isn't much of the original 1876 equipment left. The light was lit in 1876. It was started the year before, apparently. I think the lighthouse was built because this was one of the major exporting areas for fish, to the Indies and Spain, and places that used salt fish years ago.

I think it was realized very early on that there were not adequate warnings around here for ships to safely come into Twillingate Harbour. There were large ships coming and going all the time during the shipping season.

The light was turned by weight-driven clockwork. Weights were cranked up to the ceiling of the first level and, as they dropped, they turned a turntable with kerosene lamps and the lens.

It appears most of the materials came over from England. Even if they came out of St. John's, they probably came over from England to St. John's and then they were dragged up over the cliffs here. The remnants of the landing area are still down there.

This was probably one of the best-kept lights, up until the numbers of lightkeepers were downgraded from 24-hour watches down to two and now down to one. You can't keep a light with one person like you can with three. I get called down at odd hours, when the light is out, or when the fog alarm is not working. I can't know about that when I'm home.

THE FOGHORN

I DO NOT TURN ON THE FOG ALARM ANYMORE, unless the automatic system fails. It comes on automatically. The fog alarm is controlled by a fog detector. There's a beam of light fed out to be reflected. The more light reflected, the lower the visibility. When it gets down to about two nautical miles the system goes into standby, and five or six minutes later, the system fires up.

They had diaphones here up until some time into the '50s, '60s. They were just huge devices that provided the sound that deafened most lightkeepers that worked back in those days. The sound is what's caused most of us who worked in the system to have serious hearing problems. I too have a serious hearing problem. My wife says I'm as deaf a doorknob. And that's a fact.

The diaphones were driven by a compressor. As the sound trailed off, it made what's called a grunt. As the piston came to a stop, there was a grunt. That's what they called the sound. The Fishermen's Broadcast still has the sound of a classic old diaphone in the introduction.

It looks like lightkeeping may have a new lease on life. It has now been confirmed that the 24 light stations in Newfoundland as well as 27 in BC will remain staffed by lightkeepers. — G. Cranford

PADDY McCARTHY

THE WRECK OF THE *FLORIZEL* (1918)

Patrick "Paddy" McCarthy was coming out of mass on a Sunday morning when he heard about a shipwreck. He was living in Renews, Newfoundland.

I WASN'T VERY OLD. I was only 14 years old. After coming out of mass, everybody heard about the *Florizel*, which struck ashore on Horn Head, Cappahayden. There wouldn't be a heck of a lot of ways to get the news then, but I suppose the Goodridges had a telegraph office or something like that. All hands went up to see her then.

My father and I went up on the horse and slide. I suppose it was about eight miles from Renews to Cappahayden. It didn't take us long, about three quarters of an hour. Then we had to walk to Horn Head, so we left the horse in Cappahayden and walked up. That would be all of half an hour. Maybe you'd do it quicker when you were serious, rushing. Anyway, it was half an hour.

It wasn't very nice, what we did see. The *Florizel* was out on Horn Head Rock. The stern half of her was down, but the bow part was up. When the sea rolled in, it would roll right over her, even over the bow section.

The few people who were aboard her were in the Marconi room, right by the funnel. Just as they'd open the door you'd see their hands waving. Not too often, but any chance they got, you'd see them wave. Then you'd know there was someone alive. But with regards to getting to her, it was as good as trying to climb to the moon.

It started to get nice and fine. The sun came out and the wind died right down. By 2:00 it got to be a perfect day, with not a breath of wind. Soft. You knew it was calming down a bit, but on Horn Head you could hardly notice it because of the shoals. It was awful. The seas were funnelling in. But everywhere else along on the shore you knew it was smoothening down.

HELPING WITH THE RESCUE

I WAS AT THE RESCUE MYSELF! There were 11 or more dead bodies driven in there, and you'd take them up and bring them into Cappahayden Station. That was the only place suitable to bring them. The train was running a scattered time there.

There were places on the shore you couldn't get to, it was so rough. But when a body drifted into any sort of a cove or a half-smooth place, you had to take them out of the water. You'd bring them up from the beach to the road. Then you put them on the cart and took them to the station.

I often remember the woman that I brought in. That was Mrs. Butler. She belonged to the east end of town [St. John's]. I didn't know the Butlers, but they said that's who she was. She had on a brown fur coat. That was all that she had on her.

And then there was a man from St. John's whose last name was Snow.

When it got dark, I stayed in Cappahayden, because I had an uncle up there. Then I came home with the horse the next day, Monday. My father stayed up there.

In her book A Winter's Tale: The Wreck of the *Florizel, Newfoundland writer Cassie Brown lists the names of those people whose bodies were recovered. Among them were Mrs. William F. Butler, aged 40, and Mr. Fred Snow, aged 22, both of St. John's. — G. Cranford*

MARY (WALSH) McKENNA

TIDAL WAVE: AT LORD'S COVE

Mary McKenna now lives in Halifax where I visited her. This is the first part of her story about the amazing things she saw happen during the tidal wave in 1929.

I WENT OVER TO ST. PIERRE when I was 13 and I worked at a hotel. A woman had three children for me to take care of. I used to go back to Lord's Cove in May because my father needed my help. His name was Jim Walsh. I would work with him during the summer and I was there late in the fall when the tidal wave came in.

THE EARTHQUAKE

I WAS COMING HOME FROM THE STORE when I felt the earthquake. I was holding a package and my father's wallet. I was just shaking, because there was nothing to hold on to.

Your whole body shakes, especially your knees, when you're standing still. You don't know if you should move or not. It was November. The ground could have had a little frost in it, but I doubt it. And I was standing there, shaking, like everyone else.

When I got home, my father said to me, "What in the heck is going on? Everything was shaking in here."

I went to look in the pantry and there were a couple of cups down on the floor. Off every kitchen in Newfoundland, in the old houses, there's a little cupboard there with dishes in it.

THE FIRST WAVE

I WAS IN THE FRONT DOOR when I saw the harbour. I still had my coat on. I called to Father.

I said, "Pop, there's no water in the cove. It's all rocks."

He said, "What?"

And I repeated it. I said, "Come and see." That's when he got up and looked out. He stayed staring at the dry harbour. Then we saw the wave coming.

People were outdoors, hollering to everybody else. That was the way you got in touch, one with the other. So they all came out and saw it. Then when we saw the water coming, everybody started to run, because it wasn't like it was coming in through the cove. It was like it was coming from the sky. That's how high the wave was. But it got smaller as it came in.

FIGHTING WATER WITH FIRE

IN NEWFOUNDLAND YEARS AGO, especially the Roman Catholics, they always died with a candle in their hands, did you know that? See, my mother was sick for a long time, and when she died somebody had to hold the candle. That was the church's rule. It was one of those old-fashioned candles. So anyway, it wasn't all burned away. There was quite a bit of the candle left at the time she died, so my father kept it.

I was still in the door when we saw the wave coming. He was in the hall. He left me and ran upstairs and grabbed the candle. He jumped in his boots and went out to the bank where the capstan was and he stuck it down in a piece of chain.

He lit the candle and the candle was still going until after the third wave. He only took it out of there when he thought the waves had stopped.

Everybody else lost their stages, dories, skiffs, and everything. Ours was still there. So of course, that was quite a thing, people coming and looking at that. We never lost anything.

The water never came up, never came anywhere near there. Father believed it was because of the candle.

IT HAPPENED IN 1929. The newspapers summed it up: At Lord's Cove, all fishing property and provisions were lost. Four lives were lost: Mrs. Patrick Rennie, 37, and her three children: Rita Rennie, 9; Patrick Rennie, 7; and Bernard Rennie, 2.

Now, when it started, my sister Katie wouldn't come away from the house. Father and I wanted to take her three children.

I tried to get her to leave her house. I said, "Come on, Katie, I'll help you with the children."

And she said, "No, I'm going to bless the bank."

Katie went out with a bottle of holy water and sprayed the bank. There was an incline there, and that's what she did.

We thought the wave was going to come up where we were, so my father jumped over the barbed wire fence. I went under, but I had this little girl I picked up on the way. Celeste Bentau was her name.

A dear little thing, I'll never forget her. She had a kind of reddish hair and she was sitting down in what they called the chip pile, where you cut up wood. When we were running I said to my father, "My God! Celeste!"

Celeste was sitting playing in the chip pile, and I just picked her up. She didn't know what was happening. Father looked back, and he was going to get her, but I picked her up and we ran.

My father helped me put her over the fence and then I crawled under it. He jumped over and tore his rubber boot. But the water didn't even come up there.

Every night Pat Rennie used to come over to Merle Harnett's. That was soon after supper, to play cards. Merle was our neighbour. People usually finished eating a little after 6:00, so when the dishes were cleared away there was the kitchen table with an oilcloth on it. Everybody sat there. Well, this was one of the nights Pat Rennie came over. His son Martin came with him.

When the tidal wave happened, Pat Rennie was standing on the road in front of our house.

The men were around talking and he said, "There, look, there's my house, and my children and my wife are in it."

And the next wave that came, we saw it coming, so we all moved back. Well, it took Pat Rennie's house out.

The house was behind a pond, and a beach separated the pond from the ocean. They used to spread their fish on the beach in the summer.

It started with the first wave. When the tidal wave came in, it went over that beach. There was a pond, a freshwater pond, that's where the Rennies' house was, back of that. The first wave took it and put it right by the shore, but nobody could get to it because they were all up on higher ground. But another wave came in and took it a little farther. The third one took it out right farther in the pond and the water was deep there.

They thought they heard someone crying in the Rennie house. It was a little girl upstairs in bed.

Father went out in the dory; he could never have done it without help, so he wasn't the only one. When they heard the noise, Father and Maurice and Clem Harnett, two brothers, decided they'd launch a dory.

Clem Harnett stayed on the land, at the capstan. He was the one with the rope on the dory. There was a big ring there on the end, just in case they had to have help.

Merle rowed and my father stood in the front. Father broke the window and reached in. Like they were saying, it was a good thing the crib was right there. He had to reach in to get it.

They always carried a scoop in the dory. I think he used that to break the window. I said to him, "You could have cut yourself when you reached in through the window."

"When I hit the window, I hit it!"

Well, he broke the window, and sure enough the child was there, and they just had time to get in before any more waves came. This was the most dangerous part.

They couldn't get that house in until the next day or the day after that. I know they rigged up a tackle with chain or ropes. I saw them with it, on the beach. They pulled the house in, and when they got it in on the land the water poured out.

They found Mrs. Rennie and the children. They were waked in the schoolhouse.

I saw the funeral go by, because, standing out by our house I could see the church. To see all those caskets coming out was a terrible thing.

I didn't go. I didn't go to the school neither, where they were waked. Somebody told me that Mrs. Rennie was in the centre and a child on each side of her and one at her feet. I heard people saying it looked so sad.

It stays with you, you know. I never stayed in our house at night after that. I used to stay with my father in the daytime, but I used to go to Katie's and sleep. I couldn't stay there. I've been back several times and I didn't stay there.

Even when I didn't sleep at home in the house I didn't sleep well.

And I think it upset people for years. I don't sleep good now. On Young Street, here in Halifax, I would wander around half the night and sometimes set a pillow on the radiator, sitting like that.

It's an awful feeling to go through an earthquake. It was only two hours afterwards that the wave came and I don't think anyone knew there was a tidal wave after an earthquake.

Afterwards the cove was never the same, I think. A lot of people noticed it. What I mean by that is, it seemed that when there was a heavy sea there were no waves. It was like there was no bottom in the ocean.

I said to my sister Katie that at night I hear the noise. She said, "Yes, but down farther you could hear it more."

I said, "What does it sound like to you, Katie?"

"It is like there's no bottom."

So I don't know. It is strange, isn't it?

To read Margaret Rennie's recollections of her experience at the time of the tidal wave, please go to page 167. — *G. Cranford*

MAX McLEAN

FATHER SHOWED ME EVERYTHING

Max McLean is one of the best-known seniors in Northwest River, Labrador. He is very active as a volunteer in his community. A man of many skills, he fondly remembers his days in the woods trapping for furs.

FATHER'S NAME WAS Murdoch McLean. His home was in Kenemish, which is 13 miles across the bay there.

In my day, trapping was a living, and when you became 14, you helped to make money for the family. I was 14 when I went trapping. You were compelled. I went to school in Northwest to grade nine, and then I went trapping.

Father showed me everything I had to know. He was a great old fella to travel with. He never got excited, but was very cool about everything.

I found that the fall, up until Christmas, was the best time to get around. We had part of it in canoe, and part of it walking. We used the canoe until we had to give it up. We watched our chance, and used the canoe because it was faster.

Father and I got dumped once. We were running down Seal Lake and one of those flash storms caught us. We had to watch the wind, because it was usually stormy in the fall. This happened in November, with a real cold wind.

We were a good half-mile off shore when she started taking water. He just kept her straight and got in around the lake. She didn't sink. We were taking on water, but we didn't tip over. When we got ashore the pots and pans were floating around in the canoe.

Fresh water can come up awfully fast. We never did it after that.

The only way I could keep up walking with Father was when he'd light his pipe. He was always ahead of me, a real fast walker on snowshoes. Then he'd stop and he'd light his pipe. I'd catch up with him, but not in time to have a spell.

I would hope he'd light his pipe again!

FATHER WAS TOUGH

TILTS WERE JUST LOGS, trees squared on the inside. We took the axe and squared them up. That would make it lighter inside. Outside, the bark was still on it. Sometimes the roof was moss. If you were in a place where you could get good birchbark, you'd use that to keep the roof tight.

We had a log bed with brush on top of it. Father never used a sleeping bag in his life. He never covered up in his life, not even in tent. He used a caribou skin and a blanket to lie on, that's all. And his clothes. You didn't see too many people like that.

He kept a fire going all night. Father would wake up when the fire was almost out, put more wood in, and light his pipe. Then he'd lie down and sleep while the fire was going. He had a routine there that he would do all night.

In my day, trapping was a living and when you became 14 you helped to make the money for the family. I was 14 when I went trapping. We were compelled to help the family as soon as we could.

I went to school in Northwest before I went trapping. I was one of the luckier ones. I went to grade nine, at Northwest River, before I stopped. The first year I was with Father most of the time, and the next year I went on my own. I had only one year breaking in.

We trapped in Seal Lake. Seal Lake is about 30 miles long, and we trapped just about all of Seal Lake. We also had a smaller trapline.

Going in to Seal Lake, we'd leave the Nascopie River. From the mouth of Nascopie to the head of Seal Lake, on the river, I suppose, was 100 miles.

We used to leave about the twentieth of September. Usually we could hire a motorboat from here to the first portage, which was at Red River. There we took the canoe and carried on.

We'd get to Seal Lake by canoe and by portage. We had 36 portages if we went the Indian way. We got in there around the second week in October, if it was good going.

The little lakes would freeze up on us sometimes, in an early year, and we had to wait for them to thaw out again in a day or so.

We'd never be back for Christmas, not when we were on that trapline. Usually we'd leave in September and come back in January. We'd stay home for a couple of weeks and go back in again until March, when the trapping closed for most animals.

We did what we called a round of the traps, and we would come back. The stopping tilt was in the centre of the trapping line. Father would go one way and I'd go the other, but we always came back to the main tilt. My favourite place is that old stopping tilt in the centre of the north shore on Seal Lake. We always tried to put our tilts in the sun, because it was wintertime.

In the fall, we went together in the canoe. After that we would go on our own.

We had one really exceptional year where we caught I think it was 98 foxes. Plus, it might have been 20 lynx. And 40 minks, something like that, a really good year! But the prices were down then.

I remember getting 16 foxes one day, myself. That's a lot of work, to have to clean them. They're not difficult, but you'd have that many. You were walking all day until dark and you only had the nighttime to clean them. You can't let them freeze because they became too hard to handle, to skin them and dry them.

We never came out hungry. Not really hungry, but out of certain things. I've been out of flour in what we called starvation years. There was no game. No meat, no partridge, no rabbits. There were only a few porcupines and a few fish.

Some years were really bad. That's what happened to [Labrador explorer] Leonidas Hubbard. He hit a bad year. There was nothing in the country.

HILDA MENCHIONS

BABY IN A MAILBAG

Today Hilda Menchions is a senior citizen living in St. John's. In December of 1919 she was just a baby aboard the steamer SS *Ethie*. Her mother and grandfather were aboard when the ship ran into a storm. Captain English, acting on the advice of his purser, decided to run the *Ethie* aground in a sheltered cove. Little Hilda Batten was sent ashore to safety in a mailbag.

WE WERE DOWN AT FLOWER'S COVE at the time. Dad worked in the Newfoundland customs office there.

Government was about ready to close at the end of the month, so Mother decided to come up to Norris Point in Bonne Bay and visit her family. That was how we came to be aboard the *Ethie*. This was in December, 1919. Later, Dad was supposed to come up on the last boat out and continue with us to Bareneed, Conception Bay.

My grandfather Joseph Batten built the Anglican church at Flower's Cove, so he was down there working. He was aboard with Mother and me when the storm struck.

I heard Mother say that she was in the stateroom, lying down. They had to have everything they could find piled up against her bunk, so she wouldn't roll out of it.

When the time came for the rescue, she wouldn't go first. I had to go before her. Of course Mom made sure that Grandfather went ashore to take me when the mailbag landed. He couldn't do anything else for me.

I did hear her say the worst time she ever felt was when she put me in that mailbag. I think it was the worst storm they had ever experienced up to that time on that coast. They had to put me down in the mailbag because you couldn't hold onto a baby and the bo'sun's chair. Grandfather went ahead, and I guess she probably followed me to make sure I was all right.

Mother never talked about it too much because it was a frightening experience for her.

I know one thing. She kept the mailbag. They gave her the mailbag and she looked after it. She kept it safe and clean somewhere in the house. She had it folded up and it was never dirty-looking.

THE MAILBAG

MOTHER DIED AND I HAD NO CHILDREN, so my husband and I decided to give the mailbag away. Both of us were no longer young, and if anything happened, there was nobody to take it. We thought we would put it in the Gros Morne National Park for safekeeping.

I gave it to them and I had the picture taken, and as plain as could be, there was a band of red. Because the old mailbags were that colour. A band of red and then bands of white on the outside.

A few years ago my husband's cousins visited from BC. We took them to Bonne Bay to see the bag. When the parks fella took it out, it was black. It looked like it had been in a coal bin or something. That's the truth. I said, "Gosh, that's not it."

Mainlanders are more outspoken than some of us Newfoundland women are. One of our visitors went along and said, "Mrs. Menchions is not very pleased about that mailbag. She says it is not the right mailbag."

That's one thing I'm disappointed about. Very, very upset.

My husband, Clayton, was a clergyman. When we lived on Walwyn Street in St. John's, we always turned on the radio in the morning for Peter Miller's show. One morning he was talking about the *Ethie*. Frank Galgay and Mike McCarthy had written the story and said there was no baby involved.

At this, Clayton jumped up and went to the phone. He asked for Miller. "That's a strange thing," he said. "I just listened to the radio. You're saying there's no such thing as Hilda Batten being on the *Ethie*. I'm sitting down eating breakfast opposite her this morning!"

I spoke to Peter Miller then myself, and I also had a call from Captain English's daughter.

I have never talked much about it at all. I always kept it to myself. Clayton often said, "My, if I were like you, I'd make a fortune, because I could go on telling my story." He was just joking, but he was right. I have always been shy about it.

Now, I can't tell you much more, because Mother didn't talk about it very much. You can understand that. I guess it brought back memories that she didn't want to remember. She had to go through quite a lot, didn't she?

She was stuck in that bunk, and they were all thinking they were going to be lost, until this Walter Young thought about the sandbar. [Walter Young was the purser, who knew the coast very well. He recommended a spot where Captain English could run the ship aground. All 92 crew and passengers were saved.]

After the interview, as I was leaving, Rev. Menchions remarked that it was an emotional event in his mother-in-law's life. He recalled sitting with her one day when Newfoundland writer Cassie Brown was on the radio, recounting the event. As Mrs. Batten listened, tears flowed freely down her cheeks.

There has been confusion over whether the mailbag on display in the Cow Head Lighthouse is authentic and from the wreck of the Ethie, *but it appears that it is. Is is clear from a photo taken during the presentation ceremony in Gros Morne National Park that the mailbag had been turned inside out, making the red colour band very clear and the mailbag appearing very clean. On display in the park, it is not inside out, so the mailbag looks very dirtly and the formerly red band is now a dark grey band, due to the discolouration resulting from it being knocked around for years in a dirty old steamer. — G. Cranford*

FRANK MERCER

Ranger Mercer's Mission

Mr. Frank Mercer now lives in Bay Roberts. His home is filled with pictures, diaries, and stories about his life as a lawman. He was a member of the Newfoundland Constabulary, the Rangers, and the Royal Canadian Mounted Police. Many stories have been written about a famous journey he took by dogsled in 1936.

RANGER FRANK MERCER WAS THE FIRST permanent police officer stationed at Nain, Labrador.

In January of 1936, he set out by dogsled to investigate an alleged murder at Okak, 100 miles away, to the north. The body of an Eskimo had been found in the cabin of a white trapper. It was believed that he was killed in a dispute over a trapping line.

Ranger Mercer set out for Okak on a komatik, driven by an Eskimo sled driver. Many storms slowed them down as they went over the mountains to Okak. They found the body in the cabin. The man had a gash on his forehead. Ranger Mercer needed to have the body examined to be sure it was murder.

The nearest doctor was 600 miles away, to the south, at the Grenfell Mission in Cartwright. Quickly, he and his driver made a wooden box for the body, put the dead man in, and stuffed moss around him. The three of them—two alive and one dead—began the long trip south to the Grenfell Mission.

When they reached the foot of the mountains, they met with many more storms, one after the other. To survive they had to build an igloo, where they waited and waited. One afternoon, the weather cleared and they began going up the mountain. At midnight, they found a pass at 4,000 feet.

Frank Mercer remembers the scene as if it were only yesterday. The Northern Lights were dancing in the sky, making hissing sounds as they swept across his gaze.

The men began to go down the mountain. The sled began to pick up speed, so Ranger Mercer cut his dogs loose. That way, the huskies would not be run over by the sled they were hauling behind them.

Finally, the two men lost control of the sled. They could not hold it back any more. It flew down the mountain and dug in the snow at the bottom. The top came off the wooden box and the corpse flew out and stuck in the snow 50 yards away.

At that moment, his driver acted strangely. The stress of the journey in the company of a dead body had gotten to him. Frightened by the turn of events, he screamed and ran away.

Ranger Mercer was now all alone in the cold north.

He found some of the huskies and went to retrieve the body. He picked it up, brought it to the coffin on the sled, and placed it inside. Using the dogs to follow his driver's scent, he located the man. The man's nerves were completely gone, and he acted like he was crazy. He was speaking nonsense and would not get on the sled. Walking some distance behind, he followed Ranger Mercer to the nearest camp.

At the camp was an elder who knew native medicine. He took the intestine of a seal and blew it up. He tied it to a stick and stuck it on the coffin. Next, he put the claw of a raven around the crazed man. He calmed down enough to continue the trip with Ranger Mercer.

It took 12 days to cover the 600 miles. The Grenfell doctor at Cartwright discovered that the man had died as the result of a fall when he was drunk. There was no murder. The man had fallen while drunk. When it was discovered that the trapper had moonshine in his cabin where the body was found, he received six months in jail.

The life of a policeman is risky in normal situations. In the far north, in the land of ice and snow, it is even more dangerous. During all his adventures in Labrador, Ranger Frank Mercer was one lucky man.

PHYLLIS MERCER

STRAIGHT FROM THE HEART

Phyllis Mercer is orginally from St. John's but now lives in Kelowna, British Columbia. Though Mrs. Mercer lives far away, her heart and soul are still back home. Her poem "Straight from the Heart" was submitted by her friend Catherine Milley.

There's an island in the cold Atlantic waters
    Where restless waves beat ever on the shore —
Where seagulls' crying wakes you in the morning
    Calling you to come back home once more.
The rocky crags and hills may lack the verdure
    Your conscious eyes around you ever see —
But your heart and soul are constant in their longing
    To hear once more that restless, northern sea.

Though the Long Range Mountains and their spreading foothills
    And icy streams make Codroy's valley green,
Your dreams are of the rugged rocks and harbours
    The wild Atlantic fashioned with its stream.
Cabot called his first sight "Bonavista" —
    And Baltimore discovered "Ferryland" —
The rugged, foggy shores of dear old Avalon
    To you, is home, your home, your Newfoundland.

You stand once more atop that craggy summit
    Where once Marconi stood, when day is done —

Before you only grey Atlantic waters —
    Behind that snug, safe harbour and the sun.
The surf rolls loudly near that hidden valley
    Where bluebells nod o'er mounds that mark the dead.
Who fought and died for honour, king and country
    So many years ago, in Newfoundland.

You turn and there before you stretch the White Hills
    Holding Quidi Vidi in their hands —
You can almost hear Virginia's rippling waters —
    From here it is a green and pleasant land.
Then in your dreams you turn towards the sunset
    You see old landmarks there before you stretched —
The old-time houses and the old Cathedral
    Of this, the oldest city in the West.

And as the sun goes down behind Freshwater
    Flooding Southside Hills with red and gold,
There's not another country that can proffer
    A sight as dear your tear-filled eyes behold.
The lights come on, reflected in the waters
    Their beauty more, by far, it seems to me
Than all your Western cities' sights can offer —
    This scene from Cabot Tower is to see.

The place so dear to every Newfoundlander
    Is not paradise with hills of green,
But the cool, salt-laden air —
    The skies above, so clear —
And childhood's memories of what might have been
    Beckon you though nature all around you
And man's inventions are at your command
    Take you home, back home, if only in your dreaming,
Back home once more to dear old Newfoundland.

CYRIL MICHELIN

GOING THROUGH THE ICE

Cyril Michelin is an old-time trapper and fisherman from Northwest River, Labrador. He has dozens of stories to tell about his Labrador life.

I WENT THROUGH the ice one morning. They said on the radio before I left my cabin it was 20 below zero. I had to go across the Churchill River. The ice was driving awful thick.

Father told us that when we go to cross the river, to be awful careful. There's only one place there you could get through. So I went across that morning.

I got over all right. I turned the canoe over. I was running up across the bight, a big cove. My dog Mooney was coming behind me with my sealskin. We used to take a sealskin in the country, for a dog to pull. You put all your stuff in that, and tied it up. Wherever you could walk with snowshoes, he could go, among the trees and everything.

I had my snowshoes hooked over my gun, across my shoulder. I was running as hard as I could. I didn't know a thing until I went right down to my neck. I thought I was done. I told Mooney to come to me. When he did, I grabbed hold of his sealskin and I told him to go. He went and hauled me right out.

Then I ran down to my canoe and turned her over and got across to my cabin. She was still warm from when I had the fire on. The next day I stayed there. And the next day I went up to set some more traps on the river.

I'll be darned if I didn't fall in again! That morning I was going across a brook and the brook gave out. The ice broke off and down I went. I couldn't believe it.

I lost my gun, but I got it again the next day. I could see it through the clear water. I got a long stick and tied a snare onto it. I hooked the gun with the snare and hauled it up off the bottom.

I HAD A BAD TIME ONE FALL when I went up the river there. The time my gun exploded. The rifle belonged to my grandmother Michelin before she died, and she gave it to my father. Before he died he gave it to me.

My brother had a cabin up on the Churchill River where he used to trap up past me. One morning I was going to his cabin to have lunch. There was a great big rock there, so I paddled out around it on the tide. I looked up and I saw two caribou just above. So I let my canoe come back down around the rock and I went ashore, and I tied her on. My dog was with me.

I had a look at them, and what should they do, they started to swim across the Churchill River. I shot near them to see if I could drive them back to my side. They turned around hard, but like a fool I had one more shot and drove them back to the other side again.

I let them get partway across the river, so that when I got to the other side I'd be close to them.

I got over. The gun only held three cartridges. One got out of the water on the bank and I killed him. I fired the next shot at the cow one. I pumped in the third cartridge, held up the gun, and fired again. I didn't see another thing in the world until I saw the palm of my hand, full of blood.

I never saw that barrel since. All I had resting on my shoulder was my stock. The barrel was gone completely. I didn't even know it happened.

I gripped hold of my hand. The palm there was full of blood. There I was. What was I going to do? I had to fix it up someway.

I paunched the caribou. I wrapped him up from inside and brought him down to my house, my main house.

I cut a green juniper and I sawed it up in junks as good as I could. I took off the outside bark and I boiled that. I used that water for soaking my hand. I got up the next morning and my hand was solid black. My little finger here, it was as black as the stove. I never felt a thing in my left hand.

In the morning, when I got up, well, I had to skin the caribou. Now how was I going to skin a caribou with one arm?

I went to work and I got a hook and I tied him on a stick. I stuck the hook onto his skin and held the stick in my teeth and skinned him with my other hand. I had my hand tied up in a sling for one month, up in the country. I could manage to skin a fur, but I had some hard time cutting wood.

When that happened I had just started to set up my traps. I only had two mink. A month later when I came home, I had 65 mink, over 50 foxes, 10 lynx, and my beaver. Even with my arm in sling that fall I had more fur than the two guys trapping below me. I had more fur than two of them together.

With my arm in sling, my dog tracked me from the shore. He would stop at every trap we came to. I'd go and fix the trap and get aboard my canoe and tell him to go. He'd go on again. He jumped across brooks and everything, he did. It's right surprising.

He knew every word I said to him. I took him up in the country when he was really small. But he was some smart.

I came home and I went to Dr. Paddon and I showed him my hand and told him what I did. He explained that I did a better job than the doctors could in hospital. It was healed up then, a cut about an inch and a half long.

I never found the barrel. It's lying in the Churchill River up there now.

FLORENCE MICHELIN

GRENFELL NURSE FROM NORTHWEST RIVER

Florence (Goudie) Michelin was born in Northwest River, Labrador. After work as a nurse's aide, she became a registered nurse. She married trapper and fisherman Cyril Michelin of Northwest River.

EXCEPT FOR SEVEN YEARS, I lived here all my life. My parents died when I was really young. We were sort of under the Grenfell Mission. They took us in the boarding school. We could only go to grade six. Old Dr. Harry Paddon said that he wanted me to go on from there. So I had to go out to St. Anthony to finish school.

Out to St. Anthony it was really poor. It was the Depression then and they were on the dole, a lot of them. A lot of them had TB. If the father got TB, he went in the sanatorium. The mother would come to the orphanage with the kids, and work.

I went to the St. Anthony Orphan School for two years. I had an allergy and they sent me back home. So then I worked in the hospital here for a while. I was a nurse's aide, but I learned everything because Dr. Paddon taught us everything in this small hospital.

Dr. Paddon asked me once, "What do you want to be?"

Because I worked in the hospital, I said, "I want to be a nurse." He tried hard to get me in different nursing schools. The year before he died he got me into St. Catherine's, Ontario. They had fundraising for me. He raised the funds outside. His wife, Mina Paddon, looked after the arrangements after he died.

ON TO NURSING SCHOOL

I LEFT HERE. I went down to Rigolet and got on the *Kyle*. I had to wait there for a while, before we got away. We had to wait for the boats a lot, you know. Then I went to St. Anthony and on out to St. John's. Then we drove right across the island on the train. It was the first time I was ever on a train in my life.

We weren't joined with Canada then, so we had to cross from Port aux Basques to North Sydney. Then we had to go through immigration.

I had over three years' training, plus making up some sick time. When the base started in Goose Bay, they paid good wages. Everybody went for the big wages, so they had a hard job to get anybody to work in the hospital. This was 1943. They couldn't get a nurse, so Mrs. Paddon asked me to come back here to Northwest River.

NURSING IN NORTHWEST RIVER

I DIDN'T HAVE MY MIDWIFERY TRAINING, but I had to go and do the best I could. I had been ward aide for five years before, and I had helped with that all the time. So I had to do the best I could. If we had an emergency, we got hold of the doctors up at the air force, or the Americans.

One time a girl broke her leg. I had just come back from down around the little settlements, inoculating all the people for diphtheria. I got back in the evening. I met Mrs. Paddon on the steps. She said this little girl slipped down on the steps and broke her leg.

I went and measured her and knew her leg was broken, because it was shorter. I got them to make a splint, from the hip down, with wood. I stretched out her leg and padded it all around. Then I sent her up to the Goose Bay hospital by dog team. You always managed. You would be surprised. You think you can't do something, but when you're faced with it, you can do it.

I fixed up somebody's leg one time. Another person I looked after was Marguerite Michelin. Dogs bit her and I had to shave her head and stitch her.

Grenfell couldn't pay very much. The first year I got $350. That was 1943. But I didn't mind that. I got all my training and all that.

But then I was on call, 24 hours a day all the year. You never got off at all.

ENA MIFFLIN

I WORKED FOR SIR WILLIAM COAKER

Growing up in Port Union, Newfoundland, Ena Mifflin met and worked with Sir William Coaker. When she was 17 she applied to work for the Union Trading Company.

WELL, IT WAS A FUNNY THING, why I learned typing. I don't know what kind of a creature I was. But when I was five or six years old I used to go to church. When I'd come home I'd put a book up on the chair and I'd be going with my fingers [make-believe keying the organ]. I never had typing in my mind then.

There was one girl there who went up to Butler's Business College, in St. John's. That was in the basement of Victoria Hall. She went up there to school and she came back to work with the trading company.

So, I said, "I'd like to know typing." But I didn't have it in my mind that Father was going to say go.

"If you want to go, you can go."

I went to St. John's in September and I boarded at 102 Merrymeeting Road. I went to Butler's Business College. This is where I learned my typing and shorthand.

AN INTERVIEW WITH SIR WILLIAM

SO ANYHOW, WHEN I WENT TO WORK, I was 17. When I went in Sir William's office, he was sitting down with the *Fisherman's*

Advocate before his eyes. I was shaking in my shoes. I was there so long before he ever looked up. So by and by he looked up and he says, "Good day, Miss Brown."

I was so frightened, I didn't know if I was Miss Brown or who I was. So he started talking to me and before I left he said, "When you go to work, if you got nothing to do, take your pencil and write your own name. Make like you are busy. Not like Miss So-and-so, reading books all the time."

That's the advice he gave me.

Mr. H. A. Dawe was the manager. But now, the *Advocate* was there, and Sir William used to send down the editorials and I used to type them as best I could. I don't know if I had them right or not. I have a copy of his bad writing.

If Sir William came down with a written note, even the men in the office couldn't read it. They used to have to bring it in to me to try to figure it out.

When I was working there, I typed it all. I made out all the bills for the advertisements. I typed out all the electric bills.

A WEDDING PRESENT

MY HUSBAND WORKED in the Trading Company's office. When we were married, Sir William had a place on Bonavista Road, called Paradise. I sent an invitation and I got a letter back. He could not come, but he sent a gift.

Sir William wrote, "I am pleased to find you dropped the idea of having Congress Hall for your wedding. I hand over my gift of $20 and ask you to invest it in a memento of your old boss. May God's blessing go with you and Gus through your whole life. Sincerely yours, W. F. Coaker."

Now, there's not too many in Newfoundland who got a gift like that from him! He gave us the $20 because we didn't have a big wedding in Congress Hall. He believed in saving.

We sent to Eaton's and we had a big box of stuff come for Sir William's $20. We bought a clock, an iron frying pan, a flatiron, and some other things.

ANASTASIA MOLLOY

THE HARD WINTER OF 1959

Anatasia Molloy was born at Portugal Cove South on the Avalon Peninsula. She was a young wife and mother, expecting another baby when the area was hit by one snowstorm after another. Getting to the midwife or to a nearby hospital was impossible.

MARCH 4, 1959. It was my sixth child, and I was having a hard night trying to sleep. I had to call old faithful Nurse Abernethy to come to Portugal Cove South. She would usually come from Trepassey on horse and slide, but the weather was so bad she couldn't make it. It was eight miles away, so she had to call St. John's for a helicopter to come to Portugal Cove South to pick me up.

The roads were blocked in the country, and they would be blocked for months at a time. There was no electricity at the time, either.

I knew everything would be fine. Albert, my husband, now deceased, looked after the children, all five of them. The oldest was 10.

When the children heard I was going away for a little while, they got upset. I was a little nervous while waiting for the helicopter to arrive. I didn't know what to do, but I had to leave.

It was around 3:00 that evening when the helicopter arrived. People came from every corner and gathered around, wondering what was going on. Even my son thought it was a flying car.

The helicopter landed in the meadow in the outer part of the cove. Albert had to tackle the horse and bring me to the helicopter.

I was in St. John's an hour later. I then had to send a message over the radio on the Gerald S. Doyle news to let Albert know I had arrived. The baby was born on March 12. It was a girl.

Every morning, after the baby was born, I would listen to the radio to see if the roads were open to go home. This morning I heard on the news that there would be a boat leaving St. John's with food for the people. At the time, Myles Murray was our MHA, so I phoned him and he said he would have me on the boat that evening.

When I left the hospital they gave me three disposable diapers, but they only lasted for the trip home. I hated to part with them. I thought they were the best things that were ever invented! But I had to go back to the cloth diapers when I reached home.

The boat was in Bar Haven. I was on her at 10:30 that evening and arrived in Trepassey at 9:00 the next morning. That was the twenty-seventh of March.

I was at home for two weeks before the roads were open in the country, but the children were all excited about the new baby, Donna. It was an experience I will never forget.

ELOISE MORRIS

TIDAL WAVE: MY EXPERIENCE

(Centre for Newfoundland Studies Archives)

Eloise Morris worked as a teacher and headmistress, and as a nurse and nursing administrator. After a life of work in the United States and in mainland Canada, she retired to Burin, Newfoundland.

I WAS IN ST. JOHN'S. That was in '29. I was born in '13, so I was 16. I was staying at the college residence then on Long's Hill, going to Prince of Wales. I went there part-time. I was taking three years music in one for my licentiate, and taking two or three subjects at Memorial at the same time.

I remember around 5:00 in the afternoon, I was supposed to be going down to the Crosbie Hotel with Eloise Hollett, who was in there with her father, Captain Tom. And I was sitting watching for them to come to the front gate.

While I was there the lights over on the pole across the street started swinging back and forth and the old pole was swinging with them. But that's all. We knew nothing about what had gone on.

It must have been three or four days before we got any news, really. My father was the United Church clergyman in Collins Cove, near Burin. I knew that he was up on high land. I mean, it wasn't going to hit that old parsonage.

We were all sent home to the south coast, about the fifteenth of December. You could go by the old *Portia* from St. John's. *Portia* used to come right around, come in to the government wharf down here

[Burin]. If you were going across the harbour to Collins Cove you got in the mail boat with them and they rowed you across there.

It was after dark when we got in. I got in the mail boat and went across to Collins Cove. There was no wharf, just the blank seaboard there. Those mail boats had keels on them, so you could not get them in anywhere close.

The mailman took a suitcase belonging to me, plus the mailbag. The other man took me. They went as far as they could go and then I had to crawl up over this 20-foot bank of snow.

I thought, my gosh, the house is way up there, up over the hill, that's where I was heading. There was a light on in the kitchen. I thought, my God, if I can make that, I'll be all set.

It took a lot out of Dad.

It seemed to be the beginning of the end for Dad. The same night I arrived, I got sent off to fetch the doctor because my father was sick. That, I think, was the beginning of the end, really.

He died in 1938 at 64 years of age, a fairly young man. He developed serious heart trouble, and a lot of it came after the tidal wave.

I know there was one case, somebody over in one of the coves, I don't know the name or anything now, but he had to be committed afterwards. At that time they required an okay from three people. I think it had to be okayed by a clergyman, a doctor, and a police officer, something or other like that. I don't know what the details of it were.

On the shoreline, everything was cleaned out. There used to be a big store, Bartlett's General Store, and that was swept up and turned right around. The front door was right up by Kelly's house, underneath the hill, on the road up there.

Around the coastline, there wasn't a fish store left.

MYRTLE MORRIS

AUNT EMILY FALLS IN

Myrtle Morris grew up on Spotted Island, Labrador. In the winter months people on the island moved to the mainland to be near wood and shelter. Here is one of her recollections of life on Spotted Island.

AUNT EMILY CLARK, my mother's sister, was going across Domino Run, in the spring. They were going over to Spotted Island, shifting out in the spring of the year. It was late when they came out. The old run used to break through and open up whenever we used to get a bit of a sea. When the dogs heard the ice cracking they scattered. Some of them turned back. The children were in the coachie box, and there was Aunt Emily, hanging fast to the end, and she went down in clear water.

Her brother, Uncle Alec, was driving. He lost sight of her, but he couldn't let the komatik go because it was tipping out to the clear drop of water with the children in the box. The children would have fallen out in the water.

When Aunt Emily would come up, she'd break the surface and she'd blow. Uncle Alec told her to catch the traces under the komatik. She caught one and the trace she caught belonged to his leader. When he bawled at that dog to go, it whipped her right out of the water. Here she was, on a piece of ice then, and she was hanging fast to the box. He finally got her straightened up.

With her help they uprighted the komatik and the dogs started to move. But that was only taking off from shore. Then they got out on the middle. They didn't know what time the ice was going to break up. They might have gone on to the bottom, but anyway, they got across.

That was really a narrow escape. Poor Aunt Emily! She was some cold when she got over to the island, I tell you. There have been so many people who fell in the water in that old run, but there never was anybody drowned there yet. And I suppose there's more pots and pans and guns and axes down in that run. With people shifting out in the spring or going up in the winter, there were some hard scrapes out in the tickle.

MEMORIES OF SPOTTED ISLAND

I WAS BORN IN PORCUPINE BAY, 15 miles from Spotted Island. I was born in 1928. Father was James Holwell. Mother was Mary Ann Turnbull.

I married Justinian Morris, from Seal Islands. That's a place south of here. We all called him Juddy. I met him at a dance one time in Indian Tickle. He was down there fishing with his uncle.

My father was always a fisherman. He used to fish in Spotted Island, but we used to move back in Porcupine Bay for the winter season. In the winter season he used to hunt and trap fur and get wood to burn in the summer, outside on the island. Father fished right out back of the island, jigging, trawling, and using their trap berths. He used to salmon-fish off the island. One of his main berths was Southeast Point, where he put his nets.

He used to have a trap berth up in Herring Cove, just right across from the mouth of Spotted. That was where he put his cod trap. And fish! He used to get some fish.

He would have two or three men with him until the boys, Tom and Hayward and Chris, got big and hardy enough. After I got big enough, I used to work in the stage too. I used to cut throats, or head the fish. If the boat was gone to get some more fish, we would finish off what was there. When they came back we would have all the fish cleared away.

Come September they would wash the fish out and put it in a pile. This washed fish was called waterhorse fish. It was ready to spread on the bare rocks we called the bawn. Or we spread it on flakes. We took it out on the hand barrow, a few yaffles at a time. We were only youngsters then.

If you got a day like this, expecting a shower, oh how we would scravel. We didn't want the fish to get wet. Everyone had to be down on the bawn then. If there was a baby, they used to wrap up the baby and bring it down on the bawn while the mother was helping.

After the fish was dried, they used to bring it over to Domino, just right across the run, to ship it. They used to stack it in the store until the schooner would come and get it, for H. B. Dawe, Cupids.

There's something else I should mention to you. My father was a dentist, and he couldn't write his name! On Spotted there was a nursing station and there was a clinic. We used to have a nurse there in the summer, but they wouldn't be there in the winter. And Father had, I think it was four years with a doctor, from England.

That is how he got his training. The doctor often said to Father, "You can do a better job than I can."

And here he was, he couldn't read or write. He used to get his supplies from IGA, the International Grenfell Association, like novocaine. He had his own instruments. I tell you what, there used to be some people that came to him. On Sundays you couldn't get in our house.

After all the week working the fishing grounds, the schooners used to come down to Spotted. Throughout the week the fishermen would say, "I'll be down Sunday to get my tooth out."

Sometimes a captain would say to Dad, "I got a couple of fellas on board who got bad teeth."

He took a lot of people out of pain.

He used to use an ordinary kitchen chair when he was working home. He got paid 25 cents a tooth.

They always ran to Dad with bad teeth, and Dad would always be bawling out to me to help. I was his flunky because I used to do all of the sterilizing.

You would see the odd one then fainting. We used to pick them up off the floor and put them on the bench. We had a wide bench in our kitchen. I would go and get the smelling salts.

He was in the First World War, Dad was. He had a piece of shell in his head over his right eye. Oh, and that was right squabby. Soft. You could feel the piece of shell left in there. Dr. Paddon and other doctors wanted to take it out. Father always said no, that it was his souvenir. It didn't bother him that it was there. He also got hit in the leg.

We had a teacher up to Spotted Island, two winters. He was a JP, and he was some teacher. He didn't have to pick up a book to know what was in it. If he was putting a fire in the stove when you were reading and you said a wrong word, he knew right where you were. There was no such thing as standing right behind you and following along with you and the book to see if you made a mistake.

There was a boarding school over here, in Cartwright, across the harbour from where we are now. I was 11 years old when I came there to school. It's funny, you know. Today I find with the children, they're always bored. That wasn't even in our vocabulary when we were growing up. We made our own fun and we always seemed to be so happy about everything. I suppose we didn't have anything, so we didn't miss it.

We would be at all kinds of games and in the summer the hospital was open. The Grenfell volunteers, WOPS we called them, would have every child on the island playing all sorts of games. They would have a field day with running and games. You would get prizes for it and of course this was something exciting, something new for the people out on the island. A game we had ourselves was down under the stage, chasing sculpins.

Aunt Minnie Turnbull was a midwife. She was married to my uncle, Mother's brother. I was with her two or three times when she was called to deliver a baby.

The old midwives, they were some particular. Firm, too. You stayed in that bed until they said get out. Of course it made a lot of sense in one way, because your body does go through a terrible ordeal.

I guess Aunt Minnie Turnbull got it from working with the nurses. She used to look after the nurses up to Spotted. She couldn't read or write either. She taught herself how to read.

Actually, I helped with the delivery of a baby who later became my adopted daughter. There were only three families left on the island. All the rest were gone in the bay, so the only one there was Aunt Flossie Elson. We couldn't get off the island ourselves right then. When the baby was born, it was normal. I didn't mind it at all.

It was marvellous, the feeling that you get, seeing what was brought into the world. A breathing child.

It is comical to think about. You know the old Beaver tobacco, or Jumbo tobacco, how it scaled? If somebody cut their finger, they would pick off a scale of tobacco and just wrap it around the finger and tie it up. That's what they used to do. I laugh every time I think about that.

If you happened to take that off before it stopped bleeding and it got infected, they would have a different remedy. They would have to make a bread poultice and put it there to clean it out. That is what they used to do for infections.

For a cough they used different things, but molasses was always used. Sometimes they put kerosene in it, and white liniment. They let it boil and took it off and let it cool down. They used to only give you half a teaspoon. It was good, too! I suppose the molasses was smooth and sweet to your throat. I don't know what it did, but I know it was really good.

If you had a chest infection they would always steam you with Friar's Balsam or Vicks. They'd put a towel over your head with the container in front of you. It would almost smother you when you

inhaled that, but it was good. They still use that today, only they use it in a different manner.

I had an aunt who died with that old Spanish flu. She was in Open Bay. There was a lot of people who died up around the coast, up the shore. I believe there were four or five that got buried in the one grave.

It was bad. There were quite a few people who died.

I remember Aunt Charlotte Davis. I think she buried her father and mother. She was the only one left.

In the spring we children lived at the beach. You'd get your mussels and your wrinkles. Of course we used to be able to kill all kinds of seabirds for food.

I tell you, my mother used to do some queer things when it came to the cooking. In the spring of the year, the ducks were fat. When she had the ducks on, cooking, she would drain off the grease and keep that in a jar. That's what she used to use for grease, like most people used butter. In buns and puddings. And she used to make cookies and cakes with it and you never tasted anything so marvellous.

There were nine of us and she used to stretch it. There was nothing wasted, I tell you, in our house.

We never had much. We had flour and molasses, but nothing else. The only thing with Mom, she used to have a garden. In the fall of the year we took fresh vegetables up in the bay. She also pickled turnip tops. In the spring, when we came back out to Spotted, we would have the pickled ones.

I guess we were a lucky family. We were, compared to some poor beggars.

There was this family in particular who was poor. This little boy came to the house one day when we were having dinner. Whatever we had, we shared. Mom said to him, "Would you like to have some dinner?"

He said, "Yes, ma'am."

He said to my brother, "Mom and they got nothing for dinner, not even a bit of 'lassy bread."

We couldn't believe it, so Mom asked him if that was true. After all the family was fed and he had his dinner, she put what was left into a container to bring up to them. That was true. They didn't have anything. It was heartbreaking. We couldn't get over it. And here was Mom, with puddings and everything all cooked up for our Sunday dinner.

Of course we always had a wild bird or something like that cooked up. These days you could be starving for a bird and you can't get one. I almost forget what they taste like. It makes me mad, that does.

One thing we never did was kill birds just for the fun of it. If some of the old fellas caught the young boys out with the gun firing at beachy birds, they got after them to quit.

You'd have bread. Mom used to make the hops for making bread. If you made a bread today and you never had any yeast left, you pinched off a ball about so big and you'd leave that one as a leaven. When you make another bread, you put that in soak and put that in the bread that you were going to mix and it would rise up. That's what we used to do when we couldn't get yeast. But they used to have hops, and they used to make bread out of that. We would never be stuck for bread.

We always had hens. Mom used to be some particular over her hens. She would have six or seven hens. The dogs got at them and left us with one! They got out of their pen that they had. The dogs weren't chained up like they are today. Oh my, she was some mad that day.

Mother had a garden. It wasn't a big garden, but it was one of the biggest on the island. All along one side were potatoes. There were two beds in the middle, which was cabbage. You dared not touch them. There would be great big heads of cabbage, turned right in, they were that big. Along another way were turnips, turnip tops. Over in another corner were beets, radishes, and carrots, but they didn't grow very big.

The first time she ever tried potatoes was really laughable. We got a full sack of potatoes, now, mind you, that included the little small ones. She even kept them. She had them in another bag, but some of them were big enough. We used to have them with fresh vegetables up until Christmas.

When we saw the first spring boat coming around Domino Point, oh boy, that was a happy day. On the boat they would be just as happy, because for trading a bucket of vegetables they got a meal of seal. Oh my good gracious, they used to have some good feeds. In the spring of the year it was really something. It was like you were going to live another year.

It's really funny how you can manage with so little sometimes.

MARION (KELLY) MOULTON

TIDAL WAVE: KELLY'S COVE

Marion Kelly was 13 years old when the tidal wave hit. It happened on a Monday, a beautiful day for washing clothes. She was living in Kelly's Cove, near Burin.

I WAS AT A WOMAN'S HOUSE to write a letter for her. She was an old woman. She was writing her daughter, in Boston, I believe. She couldn't write, so I was writing it for her. After the shock, I wanted to go home. We didn't know what to think, really. I didn't stay. If I didn't go when I did, I would have been caught in the wave, going down around the shore on the way home.

So, I don't know, I think all our lives are planned. Don't you?

THE TIDAL WAVE

SOME TIME AFTER THE SHOCK, I was at the kitchen table working by the light of a kerosene lamp. I was still in my school clothes, a navy skirt and white blouse.

That was later, a couple of hours after the shock.

I was doing my homework. I was doing English. You know the sentence I was doing? "If you do not leave the house, I will send for the policeman with that fine."

Of course, we didn't expect a tidal wave. We didn't know anything about it, really. It came round 7:00.

They say that the harbour dried out. Whether it did or not I really don't know, but that's what people said. Then it came back in.

Well, you could hear the sea coming in. It was roaring.

Of course we all ran out in the yard to see what was going on. The sea was just like a mountain coming, but slowly. That's what it seemed like to me. Right straight. There were three waves.

My little brother and sister were in the doorway. I ran and got him and ran behind the house and jumped the fence. I really don't know how high. When I got over the fence, the water was coming underneath it.

I don't know how I did it. Because Elroy was biggish. He didn't remember anything, though, he never did. He was only three and a half.

When I got over the fence, I looked back and the house was just going with the light in the window.

MOTHER AND DOROTHY ARE LOST

MOM CAME OUT IN THE YARD. I don't know if she went back in the house or not, I never knew. Mother and my little sister didn't make it. They never did find my mother, Frances, or my sister Dorothy.

It took everything when it came.

Later, the schooner *Daisy* was in here at the government wharf. The *Daisy* went out looking. She towed in a house, but it was not ours.

In Kelly's Cove, three or four houses washed out. Mrs. Carrie Brushett and her five children were in one. The first wave came and took the house and took it out to sea, and they were all in it. The second wave came and brought it back and put it on the beach. Then they all got out before the third wave came and took the house right out to sea. That's the house the *Daisy* towed in.

My other brother, Curt, was at my aunt's house at the time. I raised them up, the two boys, Elroy and Curt.

Father was down in the woods. We had a big schooner, and he was down getting wood for the winter. He didn't know a thing about it until he got home, a week later.

AMY NICOLLE

THE COW HEAD DOUBLE AXE MURDER

Amy Nicolle is a retired teacher who has a wealth of knowledge on the local history of Bonne Bay. When I visited her, she told me the story that involved her great-great-grandfather and great-great-grandmother. They were witnesses at the trial of John Pelley, who was hanged for a double murder.

I CAN TELL YOU the story the way I heard it. Sarah Singleton, or Sarah Cross—we are not sure about her last name—was working with the Bird firm at Woody Point. Now, whether she was housemaid with the family, or what, I don't know. But she was working in there. The way the story went, she had a boyfriend, Joseph Randell, and a brother, Richard Cross.

Joseph and Richard went to Cow Head where they had a trapline out. But there was another fella in Cow Head as well. Joseph and Richard were gone a long time and Sarah got worried about them.

John Paine was an agent for the Bird firm out here in Rocky Harbour. She came here to Rocky Harbour to see if John Paine would go to Cow Head with her to look for her brother and her boyfriend.

The way the story goes, they snowshoed from Rocky Harbour to Cow Head. On their way down they came across a camp and this man was standing in the doorway. They spoke to him and Sarah told him that she was looking for her brother and her boyfriend, and asked if he had seen them.

Now, this man's name was John Pelley. So he said yes, he saw them. They had been there, but they were gone in on the trapline. Now, of course, John and Sarah couldn't come back to Rocky Harbour that night, by snowshoe, so they stayed in the camp for the night.

During the night, Pelley went out and brought his gun in the camp. Sarah or John asked him why he was bringing the gun in, and he said there was a weasel in the camp.

In the meantime, Sarah was sitting over by the fire. She noticed a pair of mitts hanging up that she had knit for her brother. John and Sarah got a bit suspicious. The next morning they left and came back up again to Rocky Harbour and on into Bonne Bay. John Paine got some more men with him. They went down and looked behind the camp there and found the two bodies of the men.

Pelley confessed to the murder. One story states that they tied him to a tree, put birch rind around it, and threatened to burn him.

They arrested Pelley and brought him back to whatever justice was in Woody Point at that time, and then on to St. John's for trial.

Pelley was accused of murder and John and Sarah went in as witnesses. He was found guilty and hanged publicly on September 5, 1809, while they watched. He was from Bay Bulls.

Sarah Cross's boyfriend was dead, and while they were in St. John's, Sarah and John Paine got married, eight days after Pelley was hanged.

They are my great-great-grandparents.

FLORENCE OLIVER

STORYTELLING

Florence Oliver was born at Northwest River, Labrador, and grew up with many stories about her family. Today she lives in Happy Valley.

I GUESS A LOT OF stories were around. I remember we used to go up to our Aunt Betsy Baikie's house. She was Aunt Jessie Goudie's mother-in-law. There being no radios or televisions or much around, we used to go there and listen to her talking about when they were growing up. The stories that they used to tell us were about the animals and stuff like that. How fierce the animals were.

The men would be gone trapping and there would be only the women and the children home. One particular story this old lady used to tell us was about the wolves that used to come so close to the houses. The homes were all built from logs. They never had very big windows in them, because they were warmer without them. This time the wolves came around. The women could shoot a gun just as good as any man. Of course, they survived by that. She shot those wolves through the window. She shot them to protect her family.

My brother was killed during the war. Them times you didn't lock your door. There was no need for it. One night, during the war, we were gone to bed. First of all there was a knock on the door. Then we heard someone open the porch door. Dad heard the door open and thought he heard someone come in. He was wondering what was going on, so he got up. He looked, but there was nobody there.

He said to Mom it was nothing, not to be concerned. They didn't seem to be bothered by it. But a few days after that, they got the message that my brother was killed.

Them days, if they heard things like that, they assumed it was a ghost or token. They said it was my brother coming back to say goodbye and to let them know he was at peace. That was one of the stories I grew up with.

SHEILA PADDON

GRENFELL MISSION NURSE

Miss Sheila Fortescue came from England to Labrador as a volunteer nurse in 1949. Two years later she came on salary to the Grenfell Mission at Northwest River. She later married Dr. Anthony Paddon of Labrador. They were well-known in the province as Lieutenant-Governor the Honourable Anthony Paddon and Mrs. Paddon.

I FINISHED SCHOOL IN 1938, just before the war. The war started in 1939 and at that time you were given several options. You could go into the forces, make munitions, join the land army, or go into nursing. I went into the land army for a year, before the war, but I started nursing in January, 1940.

I wanted to take a diploma at an agricultural college, but the day the war was declared it was closed down and there was no more training. Many of the different training schools were closed for the duration, so you couldn't just do any particular thing that you fancied. You had to do something that was useful.

I trained at the Prince of Wales Hospital, and in those days it was four years' training. Midwifery was added on. You had to become a registered nurse first, and then you took another year of midwifery training. At the end of that time, if you passed all the exams, you were a certified midwife.

Then I came to St. Anthony. I'd heard about the Grenfell Mission all my life. If you were a little girl in England, growing up in the '20s and '30s, you had a little box that you put your money in for Dr. Grenfell. There was always a missionary box. That was Dr. Grenfell's Box.

I went away to boarding school when I was 11, and there was another Grenfell Box! So I had been putting my pennies in for Grenfell for years.

Then when I was in training in London, there was a doctor there, Dr. Denley Clark. He had been working on the Labrador coast before the war, at Mary's River. Now it is called Mary's Harbour, near Cartwright. He used to tell me about it. He said, "When this war is over you should go out to Labrador. You'd enjoy it there."

He was always mentioning it. Finally, the war was over, so I thought I would go and see what it's like.

The Grenfell Mission had an office in London, where you would apply and go for an interview. They told me that a nurse was needed at St. Anthony. You could either go as a volunteer, for six months, in which case you paid your passage over and you didn't receive any salary. Or you could sign a contract, I think it was for four years. So I decided to go as a volunteer.

You were given a clothing list, a list of sensible clothes to take, and off you went. They told me in London to go to Liverpool and find the right ship and go to St. John's. It was the old SS *Newfoundland*. It was very casual. It was just, "They need you in St. Anthony, and you should go in June. It'll take you about a week crossing and there should be somebody to meet you at the other end."

WELCOME TO ST. JOHN'S

IT WAS VERY INFORMAL. I arrived in Liverpool without any money for the voyage. We weren't allowed to take money out of England anyway, and I was a volunteer, so I wasn't going to receive a salary.

Unfortunately, when I got to St. John's, there wasn't anyone to meet me. My contact thought it was the next day I was coming. So I just sat there on the wharf by myself for a long time. I went back on the ship and managed to get my cabin back for another night. It was all very, very easygoing.

The plan was that I would get the *Kyle* to St. Anthony, but the *Kyle* was icebound off St. Anthony. The ice was so long coming out that year, so I waited in the Newfoundland Hotel for many days. They gave me a little money from the office on Water Street, in St. John's.

THE FLIGHT TO ST. ANTHONY

THEN I HEARD OF A YOUNG MAN who was going to fly a small plane up to St. Anthony with a part for the fishing plant there. I found him and asked him if he would take me and he said, well, all right. We took off from Quidi Vidi Lake in a very small plane. He had an enormous piece of machinery that he had to deliver to St. Anthony. It was quite a flight.

We only got as far as Gander Lake and he had a hole in his pontoon. I sat by the side of the lake while he walked into Gander. Then he came back and fixed it up and we went off again and got to Roddickton. We stayed the night there, my first real taste of a Newfoundland outport. The dogs howled outside the window that night, I remember. I had no idea what the noise was. I supposed they were dogs, but they could have been wolves for all I knew. No one ever told you anything.

We got to St. Anthony eventually. Trouble was, we were on floats and the harbour was icebound. Where was he going to land? There wasn't any water.

He landed in the bight. The big harbour was full of floating ice, but there was the bight next to it with just enough open water there to bring the plane down, very skilfully.

THE ST. ANTHONY EXPERIENCE

You were never treated as if you were a newcomer. The Grenfell Mission took for granted that you were trained to be sensible. You were an adult. You arrived, you put on your uniform, and you worked.

The organization realized that you were a highly trained professional person. They expected a great deal from you. That's what you gave.

Well, you see, I had nursed right through the war and we had a great deal of responsibility. So, I was very experienced, because nursing through the air raids in North London, you really had a very good training. At. St. Anthony you had a great deal of responsibility too. There were only four nurses and over 100 beds. There were no war wounds, of course, no air raid casualties, but it was very busy. And a great deal of TB, of course, in those days. Dr. Curtis was in charge, and Dr. Thomas worked with him. They operated every day, a great deal of surgery.

I was in the hospital there for six months and then I went home again to England. They had asked me to come back to the coast and I said I would, but I needed to do some extra midwifery. I knew if I came back I'd be alone, and I had to be really experienced in midwifery then. So I did an extra year's midwifery in England.

When I came back, they sent me to Northwest River.

ARRIVAL IN GOOSE BAY

IN THOSE DAYS IT WAS QUITE REMARKABLE, because you could fly from Heathrow, London, to Goose Bay. That Air Canada flight used to come down here en route to Montreal. It didn't last long, but in that particular year, 1951, you could land here.

I landed at Goose in the middle of the night. There was no one to meet me, of course. I stumbled around for a while in the dark. There's a graveyard up there at Goose, right at the end of the old runway where there's a number of graves of aircrew—pilots who had crashed, and others. I seemed to find that quite easily. I found a barracks and went in there and they gave me eggs and bacon. It was lovely. Then in the morning, I think one of the Mounties turned up.

We had a little nursing station in the Valley then, with two beds. Dr. Paddon, who later became my husband, had started it in a tiny building and they took me down there to Happy Valley. Later in the day, the Mission sent a boat up for me and I came down here to Northwest River.

The day after I got here, Dr. Paddon left, so I was alone here for quite a while. That's when I really needed to know my midwifery. Then I went to Harrington Harbour, which is down on the North Shore, where the Grenfell Mission had a hospital. It was actually in Quebec. I was there all winter, then I came back here.

Dr. Paddon and I were planning to get married. I went home to England to get a few things, like a wedding dress, said goodbye to my family, and came back. We were planning to get married in June, but the nurse left, so, naturally, I ended up doing the nursing all summer, because they didn't send anyone else until the fall. I wasn't really on staff, but there was no one else, so my future husband, Dr. Paddon, said, "You'll do the nursing, won't you?" "Yes." You know, you did what you had to do in those days. That was fine. I didn't mind.

We were finally married in September.

But after that, I didn't really nurse because Grenfell always supplied one. Sometimes there was a nurse who was not a midwife, so I would fill in, but not often. And sometimes there was a gap between one nurse leaving and another one coming, so I would assist then.

LESLIE PARDY

THE FOX BAIT

Leslie Pardy is a fur trapper and fisherman from Cartwright. He also worked for many years for the Hudson Bay Company there. He has hundreds of stories to tell about his interesting life. Here is one amusing tale about the Hudson Bay fox bait.

I REMEMBER ONE TIME, I was working up there at the Hudson Bay store. They had some bottles of this fox lure come in. I'd never seen it before. I looked and thought, "By gee, it might work."

I unscrewed the top and took a sniff. I figured if I could smell it at half a mile, the fox ought to be able trace that down for five miles, at least.

So I got a bottle. I came back from working and I jumped on the Ski-Doo. I went down on the hills here and put a drop to each of my traps and shoved the bottle back in my pocket.

When I came home, they told me there was a good show playing here. I wanted to see that movie bad, so after supper I hauled on my parka. It was fairly new. I struck off for the place they were having the movie. By God, the guy who was sitting next to me, didn't he stink. It got me so bad I moved up two rows of seats and sat down. And God, it was worse there.

I put my hand in my pocket to get a handkerchief or some darn thing, and my hand was wet! This was the fox bait. The stopper was slack on the bottle of the darn stuff, and it was me who was stinking all this time. I thought it was the other guy who was smelling, not me.

I never found it any good at all, on traps. I think it drove the animals away.

CARTWRIGHT, LABRADOR

YOU GOT MOST OF YOUR DOG FOOD IN THE SUMMER. The fish that was too soft for sale you would salt in barrels. In the winter you then soaked the salt out of it for the dogs.

There were always a few seals to be taken. That was the main food for the dogs.

The jar seals are here winter and summer. That is a seal that can chew up through the ice, no matter how thick it is. The harp seals can't do that.

Then there's the ranger seal. They're here most of the year.

The square-flipper is another seal, one of the biggest. There are a dozen kinds besides the harp.

And those beggars, the grey seal, come from Sable Island. In the summer, if one of those grey seals discovers a net with a salmon in it, that's his net from then on. He will tend it more often than you do. You will very rarely get a salmon and they will tear your net to pieces.

Usually they are too damn cute to catch or shoot. Mostly it's night work with them. They tend your net in the night. You know they were there when you go and

haul your net in the morning. There will be just the heads of the salmon left in the net.

They are smart enough to do that in the night.

My father caught a salmon up the head of Muddy Bay. We had one of those spring balances hung up on the top of the door. The salmon reached the top of the door and his tail was just about touching the floor. He was a brute, 35 pounds.

Of course the old man said there were two there. The other one was bigger. He got away! (laughing)

It is really bad lately. No one knows how many salmon we would have if not for that damn grey seal.

You might eat the first salmon you got in the spring. The salmon was your cash crop. That was where you made your money. From then on you'd be hoping for a gull to get at one that's in the net. That would spoil him for sale. You'd have him, then!

Or one that was badly cut by the twine in the net. So you take that one. Be glad of those. But you would not take the number one. That was your easiest, no, quickest way to make a few dollars.

I said easiest, but it was not the easiest way. It was the quickest way, not the easiest way. You would kill yourself cleaning your nets in the warm summers. Everything grows fast, and seaweed, kelp, and slub all choked the nets. You would hammer them bloody nets day after day, hour after hour.

But it was wonderful as long as you were getting the salmon.

I DON'T KNOW HOW IT HAPPENS but you learn directions somehow. Say you went off half a day's walk in a forest one way and then made a half-circle. Usually you can leave and come straight home.

There is no way you can go by anything. How does a goose do it? How does a salmon find his own river? It's something in nature, I think. No matter how thick the woods got, you can do that. You might have circled for half a day, but you still find home.

The north side of the juniper trees has very few limbs if they're near an opening. Limbs always branch to the south. That's one way you can get a general direction if you can't see the sun.

On the barrens, if you remember which way the wind was blowing the last storm you had, the drifts all lined up one way. You could get a general direction like that. That's about the only way.

Other than that you've got to have a good dog team leader. There's none of them left now.

A BEAR IN CAMP

I REMEMBER ONE TRIP up to Muddy Bay Brook. Trout were going in plentiful. I took my young fella. He was only about seven or eight years old. We went up and set our net late in the evening.

Next we set up camp. It was in the summer, but it gets cold in the morning by a brook. I cut up an armful of wood and put it outside the tent door in case it got cold. Sure enough, it did.

The young fella woke up with the cold, but he didn't wake me. He figured he would put a fire in the camp stove himself. He parted the flaps of the tent door, and down there where my wood was there was the paw of a bear!

He fell backwards and shook me. "Dad, I saw a bear!"

He didn't say exactly where he saw it. As far as I knew it was 100 yards across the brook. I crawled over the camp on my knees and spread the door open and stuck my bloody fool head out. I brought up about six inches from this bear's nose.

We stared at each other for several seconds. Just looking at each other. If I ever see him again I'll know that bugger, for sure.

I thought about my gun in the tent there by my sleeping bag. I was quat up on my heels, and I fell backwards and reached for it.

By the time I grabbed my gun and looked again, there was no more sign of the bear. You would swear he was never there.

THE BEAR AND THE FLY DOPE

WHILE I'M ON THE SUBJECT OF BEARS I'll tell you this. I got a little cabin over here across the bay. I use it for goose hunting in the fall. A couple or three years ago I was leaving the cabin for the last time that fall. In fact, it was starting to freeze up. We cleaned out most of the things we had in the cabin and brought it home again. But we left a tin or two of corned beef, odds and ends like that, on the shelf on the cabin. I also left a can of this fly spray.

The next fall we went over there. Dennis was the first one to go up to the cabin.

When he got to the door he said, "Cripes, Dad, your door is chewed open."

The corner of the door was clean gone through. This was the bear. You could see the black hair around the doorway where he squeezed through. We unlocked the door and went in.

Dennis spoke up again. "Dad! Look! Someone was in here. Not only a bear. A man was in here. It had to be. Look at the corned beef full of .22 bullet holes."

When I looked I saw that it had to be the bear chewing the damn tin. The holes on both sides were inward. It had to be a bear.

And here was this tall can of pressurized fly spray. There were five or six teeth marks clean through that. Now, you can imagine what happened.

We had a stove in there and stovepipes stuck up. Every stovepipe was flattened out on the floor and soot covered everything. What a mess! The stove was battered, not usable any more. He wrecked the cabin. He must have gone wild after he bit into this can of fly dope.

I don't think he was ever touched by a fly after that!

THE COLDEST DAY

I FELL IN MORE THAN ONCE. It happened twice in one day! One day I can remember, I was really sorry for myself because it was really cold.

There were two of us, my young fella and myself. On the way

down to Goose Cove Pond to go ice fishing, we played it safe. The ponds were just frozen over, so we went around them. On one side of the pond a brook went into another pond. We wanted to get across this brook and it was quite deep.

We chopped down a dry juniper that just reached across the brook. We also cut a couple of little poles so that we could balance ourselves. We stuck one end of the pole in the bottom of the brook and used it for balance. Anyway, my buddy went first. He got across number one.

I started behind, not as careful as I should have been. The stick broke off and down I went, right in the centre of the brook. I went right to my neck. I was the only one with the matches. The young fella didn't smoke and he had no matches with him. We couldn't stop and dry out, so we turned tail for home.

On the way back we decided to cross the pond that we went

around on the way in. I was damn near freezing. We gave her hell across the pond and we made it. Well, we almost made it. My buddy got up safely on the bank on the other side of the pond.

I was so mesmerized with the cold I couldn't think. I was just following his tracks. Then I heard the ice crack. When I tried to jump, I just went through the ice.

That was the second time for that day. Boy oh boy!

I didn't mind that first dipping, the first time I fell through. It wasn't too bad, but that second time! My dungarees started to freeze solid.

I was lucky. We didn't have far to come, only about a mile to home.

THE WOOLLY PARKA

I HAD AN OLD THREE-QUARTER-LENGTH PARKA, an old air force job, the real thing for riding on Ski-Doo. We were over here at North River. When we camped that night it was blowing hard. My geez, it was cold. We had no thermometer to tell what the temperature was but it was way, way, down. I'd say it was 20, 25 below, and with high wind.

I put my old parka down on the boughs in the tent on my side of the stove. I put my sleeping bag on top of the parka to keep warm. We put in a good fire.

We were taking turns putting the fire in. I fell asleep solid and my buddy did too. What woke me was my buddy coughing. He was coughing bad. He was going to vomit up his guts, I figured. I looked over across and I couldn't see anything, just a greyish-white mist. Then I saw a little spark. That's my buddy, I figured, lighting a cigarette.

That little glow I saw looked about the size of a cigarette butt. That's what it looked like to me. Suddenly, I came completely awake and thought, "Sure, my buddy doesn't smoke!"

It was his flashlight. He was just about passing out. The next thing, he made a bolt to get out of that tent fast. But he took the wrong end! He made for the back end. He took the tent down on top of me and the hot stove and everything else.

Boy oh boy!

I found my parka the next morning. That was what caused the bad, stinky smoke. My parka was smouldering, right from the foot to the head.

I suppose we'd have passed out there if he didn't wake up when he did.

I must have touched the stove with the edge of the parka, but it burned a foot wide, the full length.

It needed a good patch.

It was gone, spoiled completely. I missed the warmth the next day coming home in the cold.

STORMS AND SHIPS

I SPENT ONE BAD TIME. I brought a couple of guys to Goose Bay to go to work, and I was on the way back. It was a perfectly fine day. I was driving about a mile from the shore on the north side of the big bay. Sitting on the komatik, I thought I was going to be over halfway home by evening.

Next I heard a low rumble, a rushing sound. I couldn't quite place it, so I turned and looked toward the land, and the land was gone! I couldn't see it for snow. A sudden blizzard from the north.

I had time to turn my leader in towards the land, and within five minutes I was ashore. Where we landed was right where we had set our camp on the way up to Goose Bay. The camp poles were still there and the boughs down on the snow. All I had to do was stick up my camp stove and get a bit of wood and I was ready for the night. I was glad to find that camp, because it got really bad.

I fed my old dogs just a bit of frozen food that night. The next morning I woke up and I tried to sit up in my sleeping bag, but I couldn't.

My tent door faced the bay and the north. That was okay when I went to bed, but the wind had swung around to the northwest during the night. My camp filled up with snow and I had all that weight on my sleeping bag.

I had a look and it was too miserable to do anything. I tucked down in my sleeping bag and slept until I absolutely had to get up.

After a while I started to get a little hungry, so I decided to try to get out. I got one of my snowshoes and shovelled out my tent. There were my boots, jacket and cap, and gloves, everything scattered around the floor like I left them in the night. I had to get a fire underway, dry all that out, and have something to eat.

That night my dogs had no supper. All my frozen dog food was gone and I couldn't get to cook any more. It was too damn stormy, so I turned in again for the second night.

Some time in the small hours of the morning I woke up. Everything was very still. I knew the wind was gone. I looked out across the bay. There were three separate strings of light, 200 yards apart. They looked like ships' lights, which I knew was impossible.

This was in March, way back then. There could be no boat, with four feet of ice all through the bay.

I rolled over and waited for daylight. When I looked out, there were three ships, all right, making their way into Goose Bay. An icebreaker and two freighters behind her.

Now I was being cut off from crossing to the south side. I could go back around to Goose, but it would spoil a whole day. Then I would have to come down the other side. I didn't want to do that.

Another way was to go down to Rigolet, just outside the narrows, and get across in boat. But a man and his stuff and his dogs aboard a little rowboat was not something you wanted to do. Until you're forced to.

I decided to drive out to where the ships went up to see what it looked like. When I got out there, the ice was broken up in pieces. There were big pieces and small, with snow drifted over the works.

I decided to give it a try. I sang out to my dogs. They went across as fast as they could hightail it and I stayed on the after part of my komatik, to keep her head up high.

I made it across and was proud enough to do it, too. I didn't want to go out to Rigolet and be put across in boat.

For some strange reason there's one legend the length of the coast, from the northern end to the southern part. Old Smokler. Everyone knows about Old Smokler. It seems like he was a dog driver. He had a wonderful team of dogs. Before a storm, if you think you hear a dog team coming, watch out, that's Smokler. Guaranteed. It might be a moonlit night, but a storm was on the way.

My favourite place in Labrador is a mountain to the northwest side of the bay. Barrowbrook Mountain, we call it. I don't know how high it is, but it's over 3,000 feet high, right over the bay.

From there I swear you can see 10,000 square miles of country, looking in every direction. You can see at least 50 miles to the south'ard there and 50 miles back to the north.

To the west you can see another 50 miles before the land gets too high, looking at the horizon. Out to sea to the east'ard, it's another 50 miles. That's 100 miles by 100 miles. So on a clear day you can see 10,000 square miles.

CURLEW HARBOUR

THERE WAS ONE GRAVE out there in Curlew Harbour with 29 people in it. There were two schooners wrecked there the same time, but they claimed everyone got ashore. They were on the way home and had their families.

They said when they were found most of the people were down in the pit they had dug, a big pit. That was to keep warm, I suppose, and there were men there, perished, with practically nothing on. Even their oilclothes were given to the people who were down in this hole.

I suppose these men thought they were tough enough to take it, but they weren't, of course.

They claimed they buried them all there, where they were.

THE HUDSON BAY COMPANY

IT WAS INTERESTING working for the Hudson Bay Company. That's why I went with them, as outside foreman. I handled the complete salmon deal for them. I had 12 or 15 men going around in motorboat and collecting and packing salmon on the land and shipping it out.

That was for the fresh salmon market. When that was over, we collected in salt codfish from the people all around the place. In the fall you'd ship that. Late in the fall, when the freight was all in, we would lay the men off.

In the winter I would be there by myself doing outside work. They had up to 250 nets, and I'd have to mend those and hang new ones for next year. The men would be hired back on the first of May. We'd get the nets barked and the boats painted up and ready for the water.

Some of those Hudson Bay managers down for the first time used to mess up. Especially those who were too stuck-up or a little too proud to ask someone's advice.

There was one guy came down here, Earl Boone. When he landed here he was green, but he didn't mind, he'd ask advice. That was the only way to be.

Geez, the boys used to fool him some bad. He loved to hunt. We took him one trip up the bay. We were going up for a scow load of wood. We had one of them Cape Islander boats. Earl loved to hunt, and he loved to sleep, too.

On the way up the bay, he went in the cabin to lie down on the locker. He went dead to the world, so we sneaked in with a piece of rope. We tied it around both his feet and tied it to the post that came down through the deck.

I gave him about a fathom slack.

I whispered to one of the boys, "Get a shotgun out and have two or three shots and start bawling about the birds."

Everyone grabbed a gun and they started to shout and bawl. "Look at the birds! Look at the birds!" They made quite the racket.

Earl came through the door, head first!

He just reached the doorway before his feet brought up tight.

It's a wonder we didn't kill him.

Earl did pretty damn good for himself with the Hudson Bay Company. He got to be a High Commissioner. He was from Newfoundland somewhere.

ERNEST PEYTON

BAPTISM UNDER FIRE

Ernest Peyton is known in the Gander area as the former owner of Peyton's Flowers. Like thousands of Newfoundlanders, he went overseas to fight in World War II. He enlisted in the forestry service before signing on with the Royal Air Force.

I WAS BORN IN TWILLINGATE, but I was living in Grand Falls when war was declared. I was sitting in a boarding house, and the radio was on. That's when I heard the Declaration of War.

There were four of us, good friends, working in Grand Falls. I was working in the paper mill, part-time. The four of us enlisted and we all came back safely.

They weren't recruiting for the armed services, but they were recruiting for forestry workers. We signed up to go overseas with the forestry unit in 1939. After being in the forestry, we figured we could go into the forces, if we wanted to. Which is what we did.

We tried to get in the navy, but the navy wasn't hiring. The air force was hiring, and all four of us got in the Royal Air Force.

We had foot drill down in Blackpool, England. After that we got shipped to the same air base. It was in 1940, and Hitler was trying to knock out the air force. We got bombed just as we got off the truck at the base.

One of the buildings was knocked apart. Some of the hangars were damaged. We had to crawl under the buildings while they machine-gunned us, flying over. That was a baptism under fire.

Our first training was just as ordinary soldiers. We were given rifles, and we had to patrol at night, between air raids.

I started out as ACII. Aircraftman Second Class. That's as low as you can get. The next thing I did, I volunteered to go overseas, from England. I was tired of being at the station, doing very little.

They were looking for people to make up a draft, so I applied. When they were going along, they said, you sound foreign. I said, "Well, I'm from Newfoundland."

"Oh," they said, "you're lucky."

Now, I didn't know what they meant. I knew I was going somewhere, but I didn't know where. I certainly didn't think I was going to go to Canada. That's where I got sent. To Nova Scotia!

They were building up a training station there. I went training as a flight mechanic.

Amy Anstey and I were going together for years. She was nursing in New York, so I went down there and we got married. She came back to Truro with me. After a year, I got sent back to England, and Amy went back to nursing in New York.

When I got back to England I was stationed in Wales. I joined a Newfoundland squadron then. That was great.

As a mechanic, I did everything. Not only engines, but controls and anything else. I did some flying, but that was on test flights. We did the repairs and then we flew with the pilots to check it out.

When I was discharged, I was a Leading Aircraftman. LAC. Something like a corporal in the army.

ADDIE PITTMAN

MIDWIFE IDA (MAYO) PITTMAN

Addie Pittman of Marystown respected her mother-in-law quite a lot. So did many other people, especially women in the area. Mrs. Ida Pittman, midwife, delivered 1,400 babies.

MY MOTHER-IN-LAW WAS IDA PITTMAN. She was a Mayo, born in Creston North. She moved to Marystown and married Richard Pittman.

Richard was married before, and his wife died in childbirth. They had one son, Patrick. When he grew up he went fishing, and he was drowned and buried on Sable Island.

Richard and Ida Pittman had nine children. She's my mother-in-law, really, but we always called her Grandmother, like all the children did.

There was a midwife called Mrs. Curdeau, and Mrs. Pittman used to go as a young woman to help her. From that she got interested in it.

She went on her own after her oldest son got married. The night that his son was born, Mrs. Curdeau was sick and couldn't come. Mrs. Pittman went on her own and delivered her first grandson, Pad, Patrick Pittman. He's in his sixties now.

Then she worked with Dr. Harris. Dr. Harris came here in 1924. She delivered approximately 1,400 babies. Very, very few complications. She went and stayed eight to 10 days and looked after the household. If there were younger children, she looked after them.

Her two older children were girls, so they could help look after the family. Her husband was good in the house too, and he helped her a lot, because he didn't mind if she was gone a week or two.

Area Covered

MRS. PITTMAN WOULD COVER MARYSTOWN, Creston North and South, Little Bay, Beau Bois, Spanish Room, and sometimes Jean de Baie. But now there was a midwife in Jean de Baie. 'Twas only in an emergency that she'd go to Spanish Room or Jean de Baie.

She was a big woman, about 250 to 270 pounds. One woman told me she was so light-footed, she was the only woman she ever knew who could go up a stair and not let it squeak. And she went on horse and slide, and dory. She was very nimble, although she was very big.

In the '30s the times were so poor. Years ago they used to have beds with steel laths on them. She said sometimes all they had was an old fisherman's coat under them. She'd have to come home and get towels and bedclothes to make diapers for the baby. It was all flannelette diapers then. She'd cook for the family while she was there. Five dollars was the fee, when she got it. She didn't always get it. The last few years she got $6. Sometimes they'd offer a quarter of mutton or something.

She stayed with them, and if they needed a doctor she'd send for the doctor. He always came, because he knew that when he was sent for by Mrs. Pittman, he was needed. They got along very well together.

She not only delivered babies. When people were sick, she went and stayed up with them and visited, made them soup. When they died she "laid them out," as they used to say years ago. She'd dress them, and wash them. She was a wonderful woman.

Birthmarks

I DON'T KNOW if there was as much superstition about childbirth as there was about birthmarks. For instance, they didn't want the women to sit with their legs crossed, because it would make the birth more difficult.

She told us one instance. There was a young man who threw a clam at a pregnant woman. When the baby was born, right on her leg was the print of the clam shell.

Another time a man was lighting the lamp, and the match fell on the woman's cheek. When the child was born there was a birthmark on his cheek that they said was like the brimstone on a match.

You wouldn't want to frighten a pregnant mother, because it would bring on premature labour. And of course they weren't allowed to drink or smoke. That was out of the question then, in those days.

CRAVINGS

WHEN MY DAUGHTER WAS BORN she was always putting out her tongue. My mother said to me one day, "Addie, you must have wanted something before she was born."

I said, "I don't think so." I couldn't think of anything. I mean, times were a little better in 1948. I had everything I wanted.

So, we were talking one day and I said, "I love turbot. I wish I had a bit of turbot. I wanted a bit, about seven months ago."

Then Mom said, "Yes, that is exactly what you must have wanted." The next time we got a turbot, she rubbed it along the child's mouth. She never licked out her tongue after.

You smile and laugh at it, now.

Grandmother was born a Protestant, but she became a Catholic. She had the best of two worlds. I tell you, she knew the Bible better than the ministers or the priests knew it. You couldn't stump her on a question from the Bible. She was very, very attentive to her church.

Well, I guess when she went to her Protestant friends she said prayers that they were used to. When she went to the Catholics she knew their prayers, too.

In those days it was a terrible thing to die without having the priest give the last rites. Religion was far different than it is today, I suppose. Now, Dr. Harris wasn't a Catholic, but none of his Catholic patients died without the priest. He made sure that they got the rites of the church before they died.

A COMFORT

MRS. PITTMAN WENT IN ALL KINDS OF WEATHER. Lots of times the storm would be so bad, they had to put something over her face to keep her from smothering on the sleigh. She travelled by dory and horse and slide, and of course walked in the summertime, sometimes three miles.

She has gone out when it was pretty bad. I've heard men say that she went when they didn't really think they were going to make it.

They were pretty nervous, but she always seemed cool, calm, and collected.

I have heard scores of women, and even their husbands say, "When Mrs. Pittman came through the door, it was just like some kind of a blanket of peace came over them, and they didn't worry any more."

Where she was so big, she could lift and handle the patients so well. Lots of times she had to counsel the husbands too, because they didn't realize what their wives had to go through.

Lots of times, husbands were very upset. Of course, they were never in the room when the baby was born, a sacrilegious thing then. She'd have to hush them out. "You go on out and cut up your wood now. Don't worry about anything."

SEX EDUCATION

SHE SAID THAT when she'd bring the black bag, the older children knew there was going to be a baby in that black bag. She had to take the black bag in the room, because they'd be curious enough to look in it.

If it was in the spring or summer, she'd say, "I went up on the meadow and I turned over this big rock and I got this baby boy or baby sister for you." Of course, they spent their time turning over rocks to see if there was another baby under them!

Bill, my husband, was 10 years old when his nephew Pad was born. He didn't know any more than the baby was in the black bag that she used to carry. When John's wife came downstairs some days later, Bill looked at her and said, "My heavens, Mother, Lizzie must have been some sick. She's after losing some weight."

He was 10 years old then, and never made the connection. Of course there was nothing explained to them. They were just left. "An airplane dropped them."

The midwife would put a cake of soap on the woman's belly button, and bind her up. She put a band around to keep the stomach in. And you stayed in bed 10 days and rested. It didn't matter how well you were, or how well you felt, you stayed in bed.

A lot of the people never had any prenatal information like they have today. I mean, I had a cousin, she used to wash fish. She'd wash away at the fish, and when she'd take the first pains of childbirth, she'd wash her hands, go up and go in bed, and have her baby. Just like that. Of course, everyone wasn't like that.

We had sickly people. I think there were more miscarriages then, in a way, because people didn't rest the same. I suppose they didn't have the nourishment as they have today, and vitamins.

She lost a patient one time; she bled to death. She was very upset about it, but then again, the woman was advised not to have any more children. In those times there was no birth control or anything, and she had the baby too quick. Mrs. Pittman was very upset over that, because she really thought that she should have adhered to her advice. It was out of her control. The doctor was there. It was out of both of their control.

The baby lived but the mother died.

THE MOTHER OR THE CHILD

IT WAS A CATHOLIC BELIEF or custom that the child had to come into the world for baptism, even if it meant losing the mother. However cruel this may seem, it was the rule. I sometimes think it was a very hard decision, and one that was given a lot of thought. Imagine a mother with five children dying, and leaving them orphans. Families with many children suffered when this rule was adhered to.

I did hear a midwife say she had a case. Dr. Harris was there as well, and he came downstairs. He said to the woman's father, "I've done all I can, and I can't save the two of them."

The father said, "Save the child and bring it to the world for baptism."

Dr. Harris said, "I'll do my best." Fortunately he saved the two of them.

Religion was really a big part of the things that were going on. When he had difficult cases, Dr. Harris used to say to the husband and the family, "If you know any prayers, go on your knees and pray for that little woman."

Grandmother Pittman often baptized children. The child might be sickly when it would be born and she'd baptize it with ordinary water.

ON CALL FOR OTHER PROBLEMS

IF ANYONE GOT INFECTIONS, they'd do home remedies for that. If they had a cut, they'd put that together with turpentine.

Then they'd make poultices, like linseed poultices. Sometimes you'd have pneumonia, pleurisy stitches, and they'd make poultices out of linseed meal to put on your chest.

The women, sometimes, their breasts would rise (swell)—get infected from the milk, and they'd do the same. Sometimes a doctor would have to come and lance it, but more often they'd wring out a hot cloth between another cloth and put it around the breasts.

One time Mrs. Pittman wasn't feeling well, and just down the road here, a woman was expecting a baby. She was expecting twins, and she had other family. Mrs. Pittman had delivered all her children, and of course she didn't think anyone else could deliver them, only Mrs. Pittman.

Her husband went up to get Mrs. Pittman. She didn't think that she could come. Lo and behold, her husband went home and told his wife.

"That's okay," she said, "I'll go to her!" So she went up to Mrs. Pittman's and stayed up there 10 days at Mrs. Pittman's house and had the twins up there, twin boys.

Of course, her husband was up to the house almost the 10 days too. He used to come every day to his dinner.

CLEANLINESS

GRANDMOTHER COULD BE STERN when it came to cleanliness. She was very clean. They were more particular than they are today. The patient was washed, always, and of course they always washed their hands with Jeyes Fluid any time they could. You always smelled the Jeyes Fluid when you went in the house. I can remember that.

When Mrs. Pittman went to a patient, things weren't always sanitary. Oftentimes she would come home and remove her outside clothing in the porch. She would be afraid she had picked up something to endanger her family. Of course these things were rare most of the time. They might be desperately poor, but the things for mother and baby were clean.

However clean or unclean, rich or poor, Mrs. Pittman felt it her duty to go. Her own feelings were put aside as she went to help others. A very stern, kind, and very charitable woman. At times she was at home eating a meal, or mending or washing clothing, when a knock on the door told her someone needed her. She quickly left, leaving her own family behind. The sick and needy were her priorities.

HARD TIMES

IN THE '30s the neighbours were very poor. Every time she'd cook her meal, like meat and potatoes, she'd save the pot liquor for the next-door neighbours, because they didn't have anything. Times were pretty poor in the '30s. On six cents a day!

When she gave them the pot liquor, she also gave them a pan of homemade bread to put in the liquor to soak it up. Youngsters used to come there with no inside clothes, just a pair of pants on, and bare feet. We don't know how many pairs of socks she knit and gave to the youngsters. She was very charitable.

I mean, we all went through poor times, but I never saw any hungry times. We always had lots of vegetables and meat. We always had a cow to kill, and we had hens, and eggs, fresh butter, and milk. But there were people who never had any of that.

The youngsters used to like her because she was great with them. She used to tell them stories, tell them about how they were born. Perhaps it would all be made up, but they enjoyed it. She would tell the little ghost stories to the youngsters. They were always in awe of her because she was such a big woman.

There were some other midwives around, but I would say she was the most popular one in her day.

God bless Mrs. Ida.

GERALDINE (CHRISTIAN) POWER

STATION VOGF, GRAND FALLS, 1933

Geraldine Power is a spry senior citizen living in Grand Falls, Newfoundland. She was the first female radio announcer in Newfoundland. The radio station was located in the living room of her parents' house.

IN 1933, MY FATHER, Sandy Christian, built radio station VOGF (Voice of Grand Falls.) It operated on an assigned frequency of 1,030 kcs, with an output of 200 watts.

This station was built for my benefit, and being a teenager at the time, I had to take on a big responsibility. Just looking at the mike made me nervous. It was a tall mike and had to be lowered down to my height.

I was to operate the station while my father was at work. This was from morning until 6:00 p.m. My father would rush home from the office just before 6:00 p.m. to read the *Postal Telegram* news bulletin, which people looked forward to each evening.

The station was very popular with listeners, especially during the daytime hours, for one reason. It was the only reception they could pick up on their radios.

The people who advertised were E. V. Royal Stores, Co-op, S. Cohen & Sons, and Ford Basha Insurance, along with many spot announcements during the day and night. Phil Ryan also had an evening broadcast of local news.

Sundays my father would take over the station, and throughout the day hymns would be played.

The living room of our house was equipped with a piano, an organ, and, of course, a gramophone. We would order our records from New York. If we had saved those records, they would be collector's items. They were made from a cardboard film, shiny on one side, which was the playing surface.

I remember when they became too worn, my father passed them out to my sister. They would fly them through the air, just as they do with frisbees today.

Some of the performances at VOGF were various orchestras, such as Sammy and his Gang, Gus Power, Mrs. Little, Laura Blackmore, Miss O'Reilly, and Tom Howell, as well as many more performers and recordings.

We operated for about four years. Due to pressure and dependence on his job, and it being a heavy financial obligation, coupled with some lack of support, Father closed the station down.

I never did go into broadcasting after that, but I do have the distinction of being the first female announcer in Newfoundland.

I met and married a singer and piano player who performed many times on VOGF. Last year we celebrated our sixtieth anniversary. Gus Power is still playing and singing at the age of 87!

J. STEWART RALPH

A DRASTIC HUNTING EXPERIENCE

J. Stewart Ralph lives in Point Leamington, Newfoundland. He submitted this written story for other seniors to enjoy.

THERE WAS A TIME in my life when I considered myself to be quite a Nimrod. I owned a 12-gauge shotgun, a .303 rifle, and a .22 multi-shot repeating rifle, among other weapons.

I never did get to shoot any big game, because there were no moose or caribou in that part of the Avalon Peninsula, where I was born and raised.

One evening about mid-October in 1954, I went down to an inlet where I expected to see some geese or ducks. There was no wind blowing. The surface of the water was perfectly still. Not a ripple or a wave disturbed the perfect reflection of the sky.

The sun had gone down behind the mountains and the sky was a dozen shades of red. A few clouds were lit on the underside by the last rays of the sun.

It was a place of perfect beauty and peace.

Then, about half a kilometre away, I saw a V-shaped wave approaching the bushes where I was concealed. As it got closer I could see that the wave was produced by a little muskrat swimming towards my hiding spot.

I shall never forget the beauty of the occasion—the mirror sea, the reflected colours, the evidence of nature's life, and activity all around me.

Then, as the muskrat approached, I aimed at its head and shot it.

I retrieved the body, took it home, skinned it, and put it on a board to stretch and dry. I forget what eventually happened to it. I know I did not sell it. But I have never forgotten the stupidity, the cruelty, and most of all, the unnecessary waste of my action.

I did hunt for game birds a time or two after that, but by the time I married in 1962, I had given away all my guns and I have never owned one since.

I pass no judgment on legitimate hunters who kill cleanly and use what they kill.

I just don't do it myself anymore.

Nimrod: In the Bible, a king who was a mighty hunter.

MARGARET RENNIE

RESCUED FROM THE TSUNAMI OF 1929

Margaret Rennie was the young girl rescued by Mr. James Walsh and his friends in the tidal wave of 1929. Today she lives in Fox Cove, Newfoundland. Here is her story.

I WAS AWAKE when the earthquake happened. The only thing I do remember is the lamp went out with the shaking, the lamp on the stair head.

Albert, my brother, and Dad were across the beach playing cards. My brother Martin was with them too. When they heard the noise, they came to see what it was. When they looked, the house was gone out in the pond.

When they got me I was unconscious from the mud and water and everything else. They took me and put me down in a big tub of warm water. I think this was at John Joe Fitzpatrick's house. His wife's name was Bertha.

They found Mom and the children downstairs. Mom was found in under the table. She was sewing at the table, with the sewing machine.

Now, Patrick was upstairs in bed earlier. I suppose when he heard the noise he came downstairs. Poor Patrick, he was found in under the couch. Rita was around there somewhere, I suppose. The baby, Bernard, was tied in the high chair.

I haven't got pictures of any of them. Poor Mom. I don't even know what she looked like.

After this I went to Roundabout with relatives, and my two brothers stayed in Lord's Cove. Soon after, we all got back together as a family. There was no work in Lord's Cove, so Father moved to Little St. Lawrence to work in the mine.

The story of the rescue of Margaret Rennie is told by eyewitness Mary (Walsh) McKenna, whose father, Jim Walsh, rowed out to the Rennies' sunken house. Mary's account begins on page 105. — G. Cranford

HAROLD RICHARDS

AN ADVENTURE IN THE MERCHANT MARINE

Harold Richards was a member of the merchant marine during World War II. In 1941 he joined the ship *Kitty's Brook*. She was owned by the Bowater paper company when she crossed the path of a German submarine in 1942.

FIRST I WENT ON THE OLD STEAMER the *Meigle*, firing, shovelling coal. She got off dry dock in Montreal, but we broke the cylinder head off her engine coming down through St. Lawrence River. We had to go in Sorel and we were there two months. We came back to St. John's, and she was all lopsided. She was never upright. I think she was built that way.

When we got in to St. John's, the *Kitty's Brook* was there. This was in 1941. My buddy and I went on board her. They wanted two deckhands. What was I going to do, deckhand, after working in the engine? Anyway, we went aboard of her, me and my buddy, Stan McKenzie.

You know, I learned the compass overnight! We came out of St. John's and I knew nothing about a compass, only what I learned in the Boy Scouts years ago. She was carrying paper most of the time, but if there was a chance to get a load to bring back, you would get it.

This time, it was May 9, 1942, 10:00 in the night. We left New York that morning and came down through Cape Cod Canal. We had a general cargo of sugar and 500 tons of cement and heavy equipment. The deck was loaded with heavy equipment. They had ladders going up on one side and coming down on the other, to get around.

Ten o'clock in the night we were coming across the Bay of Fundy when this sub came up. She came up on the port side and went across the bow. She was all lit up, too. She came down on the starboard side and let us have it!

I was in my room getting ready to go to bed. I had half my clothes off. I was carpenter on her and I used to be working day shift, all days.

There was another man sharing the room with me, the bo'sun. He was lying down on his bunk. He never had on any clothes, only just his shorts. He was in the top bunk. I was in the bottom one. I never had any time to put on any clothes. I had on a pair of pants and one boot, and a singlet.

I went up on deck. We used to have a raft on the afterdeck and all the crew back aft was up in this raft, sitting down, waiting for the boat to sink. She was going down by the head. She was almost up on end then. I said to my buddy, one of my nephews, from Corner Brook, Alfred Rose, "Come on, Alfred, get down out of this. Let's go for the boats."

And he jumped on my back. Now, I don't know how far I carried him, but I went up over all those big crates and went down on the other deck, and when I got there they were trying to untie this big knot which held the lifeboat in. I went and slipped the joint and the lifeboat went out.

There weren't many in our boat, only four at first.

Some of the men were in the boat when she was lowered. I had to go down the line. I know I burned my hands. So I don't know if I still had Alfred on my back or not!

When the *Kitty's Brook* sank, we were probably about 100 yards or more away from her. It was seven minutes, from the time she struck until she went down. She didn't catch fire, but the oil was flowing right out of her, out of the stack. Everybody was covered with oil.

No Plug!

WE GOT IN THE BOAT, but the boat didn't have the plug in, and she started to sink. Leak! She leaked like a basket.

Well, with the force of the water coming in, it was a hard job to get the plug in. But we managed to do it and get the water out. We picked up one fella. He went down with the raft. He said he went right to the bottom with the ship. Now, you don't know if he did or not, but he was holding on to a suitcase in under his knees and that suitcase come back with him. He hollered out, "I'm on a raft, all by myself."

We took him off the raft, and that made five in our boat. But the other boat got away before we did. There were two boats that got away. But we never saw the other lifeboat after, until we got ashore at Lockeport.

ROWING TO NOVA SCOTIA

THEY TELL ME WE ROWED 52 miles. We were rowing from 10:00 that night, that was Friday night, until Sunday noon, 36 hours I believe it was.

We rowed towards Lockeport, Nova Scotia. The weather was calm as it happened. There wasn't too much wind at all, but it snowed that night. That was bad. The tenth of May.

I had on one boot, a singlet, and my pants. They had emergency blankets in the boat, so we cut them up and covered up. One fella, my buddy who was on the top bunk, he only had on his shorts. We had to make a suit for him.

The other lifeboat got picked up, but we rowed all the way to Lockeport.

We had one man injured. When I slipped the block on the deck, for the boat to swing out, the block hit the side of his foot and tore the side off it. Every time I saw him, years after, he used to thank me, because he was getting a good disability pay.

We rowed into Lockeport. They took us ashore and they brought us to a big modern fish plant. There were all kinds of wash basins along by the wall, and mirrors and everything. We went there and washed up. We got the grease and oil off us. Then they gave us, I believe it was two hours' sleep. We went in and got in bunks, and that was it. I think it was the best two hours' sleep I ever had in my life.

They sent down a bus from Halifax. We got on the bus and they carried us up there and checked us out at the hospital. There were a few who stayed in hospital, but I got away. I never had any injuries or anything.

They sent us home and gave us a certain length of time off. Then they called as soon as there was a vacancy on another ship.

CAPTAIN JOHNNY RUSSELL

THE GHOST OF AUNT SALLY BARKER

Captain Johnny Russell is from Bonavista Bay. In his eighties he wrote a story of his life: *Memories of a Lifetime*. One day, a man he knew well told him how he met the ghost of a woman who was lost berry picking.

THERE WAS AN OLD WOMAN up in Open Hall who left her house one evening in September. Aunt Sally Barker was her name. This is a true story. This happened in my day.

Her house was near the centre of the village. She said she was going into her garden to pick a few berries. The berries were just starting to get ripe, around late September. So she left her house with her jug or dipper to put her berries in, about 3:00 in the afternoon.

It was getting up in the fall of the year, so it got dark earlier. Anyway, she went on. Suppertime came with no sign of the old lady, and she didn't come back that night.

She lived with her niece and nephew. They didn't know what to think of it. It was really too late to go look for her, but they went in where she was supposed to be. Of course, there was no sign of her. And from that day to this day it never was known what happened to Sally Barker.

Later in the fall, in November, we used to get our wood. We'd go in on King's Cove Road and have a day cutting and sticking up. By the time we walked in it was almost time to boil the kettle.

This man went one fall morning. He had a spurt cutting and

sticking up, as the saying used to be. He boiled his kettle and had a lunch. The days were getting short.

The outcome of the story was, he stayed down in the woods a little bit too long. When he walked up the woods path to the main road going from King's Cove to Open Hall, he stopped. The road had a bit of a straight stretch to it.

He put down his axe to fill his pipe. He filled his pipe, and when he went to put his hand in his pocket to get a match, he looked. He saw a woman coming.

This is true. The man told me, sitting down in his own kitchen, these exact words. "I said to myself, now, I'll have a bit of company."

It was what we called duckish, dark. He said by the time he got his pipe lit, he figured she would be getting a little handier toward him. But he looked and she was still in the same place. She never moved.

He said, "I put my axe on my back and smoked my pipe and dodged on. When I started to walk, she started to walk, too. I walked up to what we called the crossroad. When I got up on the hill at the crossroad, I looked around. She was stood up and she let out a loud roar. No, it was more like a screech, the screech of a woman."

And that's all he saw of her. She more or less vanished.

He began to realize that it was something unreal. He was a good two miles from home. He told me, "Buddy, it was the quickest time that ever I came out the Open Hall Road."

He always said, from that day until the day he passed away, that it was Sally Barker.

She had on the same kind of a dress she used to wear. The same kind of a rig.

Yes, boy, he always claimed that he saw Sally Barker, whether it was her spirit or whether it was her in reality.

The man who told me this was Kenneth Hobbs.

GORDON SHEARS

THE CEMENT SINK

Gordon Shears operated sawmills all his life. When something broke, he fixed it himself. He was always making parts for engines and liked solving problems to make life easier in Rocky Harbour, Newfoundland. One day he decided to build a cement sink.

WE LIVED IN A LITTLE HOUSE that I'd bought. It was down here under the hill. A one-storey house. And we didn't have any water in it or anything. You heard about the *Raleigh* going ashore in Forteau, the big old warship. I bought some pipe from a man in L'Anse au Loup, that he got out of the *Raleigh*.

I bought 100 feet of one-inch pipe out of the *Raleigh*. I think it was $5. And I brought it home to put water in the house. They were all cut off on the ends, broken off, so I sawed them off square and I threaded them with a hacksaw and file. I put three threads around each one, and forced a coupling on it.

There's a brook running down there now. I dammed off the brook to bring water in the house. So, I got that done, but I didn't have a sink. I couldn't afford to buy one. My brother Jim, he was used to using cement.

He said, "Make one out of cement."

I said, "I don't know how to make it."

He said, "We'll make one. I'll make the form for you."

So he helped me make the form. We made the sink with cement. A hundred and fifty pounds of cement I put into it. We were tickled to death. One end was big, for washing clothes. My wife could put the scrub board down in the sink and wash the clothes in one end. The other end was for washing dishes.

So, everything was the best kind. Sometime in February, the weather was pretty cold.

We just had a stove in the house and we used to let the fire go out when we went to bed. So this night, it was so cold, it was about 20 below zero. I said, "They tell me you should let the water run, so it won't freeze. I think we had better let the water run tonight."

So we went to bed and left the water running.

Some time in the daylight, I woke up. The water was stopped running. I jumped out of bed, and when I went to the door I struck the ice.

The outlet in the sink froze up and then it overflowed. The water ran down over the sink onto the floor, and it froze. Over by the sink there was about two inches of ice and it spread over the floor and over to the hall door.

The floor was all one glare of ice. Almost five inches thick in places!

That was Sunday morning. We had to get up to get the axe and the shovel and chop the ice off the floor and shovel it out.

IRIS SHEARS

CORMACK, NEWFOUNDLAND: PART I

Iris Shears lives in Cormack, Newfoundland. In November of 1947, Iris, her husband, and their little baby left Rocky Harbour to drive to their new home. Cormack is 18 kilometres north of Deer Lake.

MY HUSBAND WAS an ex-serviceman, navy. Royal Navy. When they came home from overseas, veterans had choices. There were different projects that each one could choose. Cormack was built up as a farm settlement for veterans. Some more went fishing.

There were three of us in the cab of the pickup truck. And the road snowed in behind us as we were coming. The next day everything was snowed in. You couldn't get through the country. That was the last time we could have gotten through that winter. From here to Deer Lake, the road was plowed. It was a dirt highway and icy as old heck. We came here the eleventh of November.

What they did was build up the shell of a house. Clapboard on the outside. There was nothing else done inside. No insulation. No basement. There were windows, but no storm windows, nothing like that. As a matter of fact, you wouldn't even call it a cabin. A log cabin would have been a whole lot better.

They were shells, clapboard on posts. There was a cement chimney which cracked. There was no basement under the house. It used to heave, and of course, the chimney would crack and the flames came out through the sides. There were quite a few houses burned up here the first years that we were here.

The baby was six weeks old when we came here. And we had this little wood stove that burned only birch rind. I had nails in the ceiling. I would hook the quilts in them and I would enclose the stove and get inside the quilts. That was the only place warm enough to give her a bath or change her diapers. Outside of that, it was cold. There was frost everywhere. But the thing was, she didn't have a cold the whole winter. That was the surprising part about it. Because she was so used to the cold. When she would wake up at night, her hands would be blue.

A Poor Winter

YOU KNOW, I'VE TRIED to think about how we lived. I don't know how we did. There was no income. Roland was cutting railway ties that winter. I remember that he had $18. That's all the money that I remember having that winter. We stretched the $18 over the very basic things. Flour wasn't as expensive then as it is now. There just wasn't anything.

Roland would catch rabbits. We had rabbit, bottled rabbit. And I used to say then, if ever I get to the point where I don't have to eat rabbit, I'm not going to eat it. And I don't. I got so turned off rabbit I haven't eaten it since.

The next year we kept a pig. We'd kill it in the fall, since by then it was cold. It was cold those winters. It wasn't like it is now. We had cold winters and hot summers. Summers were like it is now. In fact, there wasn't any water, because the wells would go dry. We had to dig the wells by hand. And we could only go down a bit below water level, so when the weather was like it is this summer, the well went dry.

And that is what it is all about. We didn't have anything.

When this settlement was originally planned, it was planned so that people were closer together. A house on either corner. But there was nothing like that done.

I had just come from a fishing village where all the people were together. Here there was no social life, no support, nothing. My parents were up at Daniel's Harbour and I was here, in the bush, in the woods.

There was nobody. There were no lights. And you didn't see anyone. So there was a lot of fear. As a matter of fact, I built up a lot of fears, and after a month or so I couldn't go outside during the day.

That's when I learned to fight fear. We had a clothesline, but I got to the point where I couldn't go out and put clothes on the line during the day. Because this was all new to me. I wasn't used to living in the bush, with nobody around. I developed a fear of the unknown. It was a deep-seated fear that I had to fight. So I fought it, and it made me a stronger person.

CORMACK, NEWFOUNDLAND: PART II

After a hard winter settling at Cormack, Newfoundland, Iris Shears got over her nervousness at being isolated. She then looked to the spring and the clearing of the land. It was difficult, with little money and little equipment. She was lucky that the farm was on a main road. By growing the right things, she could sell them at the roadside and in Deer Lake and make a living.

WE HAD TWO ACRES CLEARED around the house site, and then there were eight acres in on the back, cleared, but it's all grown over now.

We were supposed to be farming, but there wasn't anything to do farming with. We were given a couple of pieces of horse equipment, but no horse. I think in the next year they allotted you a few dollars for a horse, if you wanted.

We bought a little Cub tractor in 1948, with some little plows and things like that on it.

There was nothing cleared in '47. Our land was cleared the next year, in the spring of 1948. It was 1949 when we got the $800, two years after we got here. We were growing a few vegetables by that time.

A lot of the hard times I've blocked from my memory. I don't want to remember. I can't remember because it was too harsh. Some of the things I survived made me stronger for it. There are a few other things I wouldn't put down on paper anyway.

We didn't know any different. It was a thing where ignorance is bliss. But it's only in these late years that I look back and see what happened. For four and a half years that Roland went overseas he got $800. And this land, that was nothing.

Government cleared this 10 acres of land with a bulldozer. They took all the topsoil off and pushed it all in the back. Beautiful raspberries grew there, but there was nothing left on the land but the sand and the pug. Now, build it up and try to get something growing in it!

Britain wasn't very nice. I've learned what the Canadian government did for their servicemen and it just makes me boil. We were here for 18 years without electricity. We had kerosene lamps.

There was nothing. Try to get over the highroad if you could. It took a tow truck to get you out of the ruts.

Well, what I used to do, I fed the family off the gardens. I would market in Deer Lake and set up a highway sign here. A lot of people used to travel through here at that time, to go to Big Falls. It was a well-travelled highway. So anything that I had to sell, I'd put a sign up on the side of the road and sell it.

Most of the farmers were down on the byroads, but I had the main road to myself. So anything that I could grow, I could sell it.

I grew things for the early-market garden. Greens and rhubarb, lettuce—some things that I could sell early in the spring.

I grew a lot of strawberry rhubarb, sometimes three pounds to a stalk. It was huge. Colemans in Deer Lake used to take it. It was surprising how much you made.

We built a barn and we kept hens. We went into the hens five years after.

Potatoes and the rough crops were only for our own consumption. We didn't have it for sale.

And then I had the strawberries. They came when Rodney and Joy were big enough to go in the fields with me. They must have been 10 or 12 when I started with the strawberries.

Pansy, our first child, was six when we had two more right together. There were only 14 months in the difference between Rodney and Joy. But there wasn't any school, not out this way. There was a school five miles inside. Pansy started school when she was seven. I taught her kindergarten and grade one and she just took her exams in the spring. By the time she was seven there was a school two miles in the road, so she went to grade two. But she had to walk the two miles. The year she took grade nine was the first year we got the buses.

I was born with this gift of sewing. I passed the genes on to my two daughters as well. I was born with it. I could take anything as a small child and cut a pattern out of it. When I was 10 I made myself a princess-style coat. I would do sewing for my sisters.

I had an old treadle sewing machine that an aunt in Corner Brook gave me. I used to take in things from other people, like a coat or dress, rip it down, and make clothes for their children. I would make a few dollars that way. As I go talking now, things like this come to mind.

When I think back, sometimes I say why did I stay here this long?

It wasn't fun living here, but we learned to survive. I'm a stronger person for it and I think the children are, also.

They really didn't know any of the tough times. They didn't realize it, because children didn't ask for money. They ask for security and love. Quality time, that was the thing that my children had. That was all they had. The first three years of Pansy's life she spent in her playpen, out in the garden with me.

But it built a strong back. If I could go back to those years, with some of the knowledge that I have now, I would go back. I would change a lot of things. The possibilities and the opportunities were there. All you had to do was take it, but you needed help. It's the same thing today. There are opportunities, but you have to go for them.

After the children got older and went to school, I got a job at Deer Lake. So, I did gardening here, and worked in hotels in Deer Lake, until I left in 1977.

Iris Shears moved to Fredericton, New Brunswick, in 1977, where she worked as matron of a senior citizens' home. At the same time she owned and managed her own tailoring shop and bought several town-houses and became a landlady. Since then she has returned to Cormack, where she lives with her daughter Joy.

ENID SMITH

THE GULLY

Mrs. Enid Smith married Canon Tommy Smith, a minister for the Anglican Church. Their second parish was at Salvage, Bonavista Bay. Of all the places they lived, Salvage was Mrs. Smith's favourite. The Smiths moved to Salvage in 1948. It was a big change moving from a city church to an outport church.

WE WENT OVER to the rectory. The parishioners were all there. The fire was lit and it was enough to bake you.

The minister was always called "parson." One said, "Do you think we got everything for the parson?"

They all started to think and count up what they put in. They all got talking. They had food stored away. Everything had been cleaned and papered. They had our beds made.

Bejeepers was a term they used to use. Not everybody, but this old gentleman did. He piped up. "Bejeepers. We forgot the gully!"

I looked at Tommy, and Tommy looked at me. What was a gully? We dared not go asking questions. We just pretended we knew.

The first thing in the morning, Tommy said, "Enid, have you been thinking what a gully is?"

I said, "I really don't know what it is."

Then the old gentleman came in.

He said, "Parson, I got the gully, but she got to be plimmed first. It will take about three days, but you will be all right until then. I got it plimmed, but she's got to dry out."

The next day, he came in and reported on the gully. He had the cover made. We still didn't know what it was.

The last thing was the "paint job."

Still, we couldn't figure it out. What had to be plimmed? What had to have paint?

After three days, he said, "I got her finished. She's out on the brudge."

That meant the "bridge," the steps outside the back door.

He said, "Come out and see what you think."

We nearly knocked each other down, getting out to the brudge. Lo and behold, what should be there, but a water barrel!

That was essential. Everybody had to have their water barrel. This water barrel would be kept filled. In the summertime it would be out of doors. Then it would be moved in on the steps. Then as it got colder, it would be moved into the back porch.

When it got cold and everything would freeze out there, it would be moved to the corner of the kitchen.

This was the gully.

He said, "My son will see that it is full all the time. You won't have to worry."

That was true enough. He used to come and chop our wood for us. He would bring the water and fill the gully. I could always depend on him.

GEORGE SNOW

THE LUMBERWOODS, 1930

In 1930, George Snow was 15 years old. He was living in Rocky Harbour, Bonne Bay. In June he went with his father to cut pulpwood for the Bowater mill at Corner Brook.

THAT WAS THE ONLY WORK there was at that time. You had to go in the lumberwoods or you went fishing. If you made a dollar in the woods, you got a dollar. But if you made a dollar fishing, you didn't get it. You traded it. That was the difference.

I went in with my father, Edgar Snow. The camps were in Lomond area, Bonne Bay. You had to walk then. You just took your clothes in a pack on your back. You walked because there were no roads those times, only trails.

FIELD BUNKS

THE CAMPS WERE JUST LOG BUILDINGS. You had a centre area about eight to 10 feet wide. Each side of the camp was just one straight field bunk, almost like a fish flake. All on one level. There was a longer for a rail between you and the next man.

You would go and pick your boughs and make your bunk with a blanket. There were anywhere from 25 to 40 men in a camp.

There was everything in them. At any given time you never knew what you were going to run into: lice, bedbugs, crabs. You mention it, it was there. Sometimes you'd have it fairly good. There wouldn't be too much of it, but other times it would be drastic. It didn't matter what time of the year, winter or summer.

They'd dump all the food. All the trash from the camp was dumped out there about a few feet from the door. Nothing was buried, and the rats, there would be millions of them.

Usually the camp would be built by the side of a brook. That's how they'd get the water. If you had 30 or 40 men, you'd have a cook and a helper. The helper cut firewood for the stove, cut it up in stove lengths and hauled water.

Anything you wanted, such as tobacco and clothes, or anything like that, you had to buy separately. They had what they called a van. It was a little room where you could buy stuff.

FOOD

BREAKFAST WAS BEANS, bread, and tea. You'd have to take a lunch. It depended on the distance you had to walk. Sometimes you took beans, or salt beef and bread. They had that cooked. Some boiled the kettle, and have tea and sugar and that sort of thing. Any brook, you'd drink out of it. Or any hole with water anywhere, you would drink out of it.

IN THE WOODS

WE HAD A BUCKSAW AND ONE AXE EACH. They were coming in with the smaller blades, about one inch wide. Before that, they used the Simon saw, or cross-cut saw, the two-handers. It depended on the type of wood you had, but we usually cut around three cords a day. Our pay was around $2.50 or $2.60 a cord. That was just before the Depression. Then it dropped down to $1 a cord.

Our board cost 60 cents a day.

You'd get up at 6:00. Breakfast was at 7:00, to be ready to go in the woods by 8:00. You'd work until 7:00 or 8:00 at night.

Sometimes, on Sundays, we would play horseshoes or more or less lie around. You might go up the brook for fishing, trouting, or something like that to pass away the day.

FLIES

THE MOST DIFFICULT THING FOR US youngsters first going in the woods was the flies. You had nothing to keep the flies off. You'd mix something up. A mixture of Stockholm tar and one thing and another, but it was useless. In the summertime the weather would be so hot. You'd sweat so much, if you put it on, the sweat washed it off again. And the sandflies, they were in swarms, the no-see-ums, just like clouds.

After a while, you'd be sweating. With so much salt, your underwear could stand alone after it dried.

THE BUCKSAW

A LOT OF THEM used to make their own wooden frames, but most used metal frames. The company used to supply the frames. You'd buy your own saws.

You'd buy the saw and the file. The teeth were formed, but you couldn't use it until it was filed. You had to file the saw first before you could use it. It's an art in itself. It's something that you had to learn. If the saw is not cutting, you work that much harder trying to cut pulpwood.

A blade would last for months, provided you didn't break it. But it was such a narrow, thin steel. If you nipped it somehow, or if the tree dropped on you, you'd bust it off, because it was tight in those bow frames.

CHANGES AFTER THE WAR

THERE WERE NO CHANGES until after the war. I went back in the lumberwoods again after I came back from the war, for a while. There was a certain amount of change, because the companies bought a lot of bedding left over from the war years. Most camps had mattresses and had metal bunks. Double bunks, one on top.

After the war, they got that DDT. That cleaned up the lice and that sort of thing in the camps. You didn't have to go through so much misery that way.

They either had oil or coal in the wood camps, another change. You didn't have to cut wood for the stoves and that sort of thing.

PROMOTION TO SECOND HAND

I TOOK OVER THE DUTIES of the foreman when he wasn't there. That was after the war.

You'd go in the woods and place men. You would probably start off at a bog somewhere. You'd have a road so many feet wide, to the end of the cutting. The woods roads were all blocked out. Every man had a block to cut.

You also placed men in the woods when they came into the camp. If a man came in, if the camp wasn't full, you took him on. That was it. You filled up the camp, but after that there was no more hiring.

IT WAS SLAVERY

IT WAS SLAVERY. It was the worst job in the world. Because it was all contract work, or piecework, whatever you mind to call it. If you didn't earn it, you didn't have it.

At that time, too, you had to go to the doctor. If he turned you down, you didn't get in the woods. You had to have a doctor's recommendation to get hired in the camps.

Dr. Greene was always there in Deer Lake, far as I know, during the years I was there. He was a pretty good old rascal. You'd have to be pretty far gone before he'd turn you down. He knew there was nothing else for people to do.

Only the fittest survived. TB was a big problem, as well as back problems, strains, and hernias.

At first, when you were using the bucksaws and that sort of thing, you had to use an axe for trimming. A lot of people got some bad cuts with axes.

But it didn't seem to bother me that much.

THOMAS STOODLEY

RAYMOND STOODLEY'S WAR STORY

Ray Stoodley

After retiring from driving a bus in Ontario, Thomas Stoodley moved to Hibbs Cove, Newfoundland. His father was a sailor in World War II when his ship was attacked.

FATHER WAS SHELLED BY A German raider on the tenth of July. This was in the Caribbean, 450 miles east of Barbados. They saw a ship on the horizon flying Swedish flags, but she was really the German ship *Narvick*. The first shot hit his ship, the SS *Davisian*, in the bow. The wires from the funnel came down around his head.

He got his life jacket on and got into a lifeboat. The German ship made them climb aboard as prisoners of war. They were locked up with men who had already been there for one month, to the day.

The next day 40 more men were also locked up. It was very crowded down in the bottom of the German ship. They were locked in a place with heavy plank across the door, and a gunman with a machine gun outside.

On the fourteenth of July another ship came near and the Germans attacked that one, too. They were locked up right under the guns, and it was very noisy.

When the noise stopped, they were marched to another room. They told them to put on their life jackets and get ready to go in a lifeboat. They filled three lifeboats with prisoners and set them adrift. They were 269 miles from a French island. After a couple of nights they lost sight of the other boats, so they drifted on.

Father's ration was three Spillar's biscuits every 24 hours and about half a pint of water a day. They had to keep watches because the boat was full of shrapnel holes. They made landfall with only enough water for one more day. In the morning they decided to land on the beach to look for water. There was a reef about a quarter of a mile from shore. They got over it and reached the beach.

When they jumped out they were in water up to their throats. Some held onto the boat and others went for water. They got the fresh water, but it was very hard trying to get off the beach again. The sea came in over the stern and half filled the boat. Finally, they got outside the reef.

When they got out, they discovered that they had left a man on shore. It was too dangerous to go in over the reef again. Third Officer Victor Harrison tied a rope around his waist and leaped into the foaming sea and swam ashore. He tied the rope around the man and they pulled him on board the boat. Victor swam back to the lifeboat.

They were off the Republic of Dominica. They rowed around to look for a harbour, when they saw a ship coming up behind them. She altered her course and came to their assistance. It was the SS *Leif* and they told them they were 45 miles from a harbour. They climbed up the side of the ship by the ladder, all feeling very much exhausted. Some of them fell on the deck and within minutes were asleep.

Captain Wilson and his men were very kind to Father and the others. They fitted them all with dry clothes, and after a bath and a good stiff drink of whisky, they were feeling much refreshed. At the *Leif*'s next port of call, there were hundreds of people lined up on the pier to see them land. It was the twentieth of July, seven days after they were set adrift.

They were taken to a fort that night. The next day they took Father and the others to Long Beach, where it was very comfortable under the shades of big tropical trees. He always remembered the nice cool breeze blowing right in from the sea.

There, in Porto Plata, the British Consulate made plans to get Father home to Newfoundland.

STIRLING THOMAS

The IWA Strike

Everyone in Grand Falls and Windsor, Newfoundland, knows Stirling Thomas. He has been on the town council for many years and is a member of most of the service clubs. As a union man he had a front-row seat to one of the most famous labour strikes in Newfoundland.

THE IWA (INTERNATIONAL WOODWORKERS OF AMERICA) came in here with the feeling they were going to organize everyone in the province.

One of their leaders even told me himself that he was a communist. "Carried a commie card." They were his words.

"Well," I said, "we don't go for that around here." At the time I was a vice-president of the Newfoundland Federation of Labour and I was president of the Trades and Labour Council.

He told me, "We're going to organize everything in Newfoundland. Even the domestic workers. And we're going to bring the government to their knees."

They came in here and went around to the camps and offered the loggers everything. There would be more money, better living conditions, more time off, and they fell for it, like they would. There was nothing wrong with what they were saying. The only thing was, their attitudes and their tactics were unbecoming to us people.

I was working with the finishing department in the mill. I was in the core room at the time, and none of the men wanted anything to do with a strike with violence. They didn't see any need of it.

The labour activities and the labour policies the IWA had didn't belong to us. They didn't belong to us at all. They were throwing people out of the camps, and throwing company property out of the camps, taking over everything.

The police had to turn the armouries into prison camps. One Sunday, the IWA got people to come in and visit, to bring in dinners to them. What they brought in was bags of nothing. It was just to put on a show.

They had another stunt up in Badger that they pulled off. They threw a handful of nickels around a garbage container and the youngsters went after the money. They said they were eating the garbage. They were a smart group.

They had the Mounties in here. Sure, they couldn't do anything. Joey Smallwood took the bull by the horns and sent people in. If they didn't behave themselves, he'd decertify them, and kick them out altogether. As far as Smallwood was concerned, there wasn't room enough in Newfoundland for him and Landon Ladd.

If the IWA had come in here in a peaceful way and talked to us people, the union leaders, it would have been okay. If they were going to do this peacefully.

They should have kept clear of the company and the government. They should have gotten the goodwill of the men first, to get a united front. With all the workers of the Corner Brook mill, with all the workers of the A.N.D. Company mill, with the central and the west covered, the companies would have had no choice but do something.

There would have been a big income in union dues for the IWA.

I think they would have done well. The IWA could have worked with the officers of the Loggers Association. However, they didn't. It was "the hell with you" and "the hell with you." They brought in their own group and picked up some people that they thought would be of a great benefit to them, but they were no good to them.

There was a loss of life over this. There was a truck lost over on a river, and there was a man killed in Badger. They had a man taken up, but he wasn't convicted. It went to court, but it was dismissed.

The government sent police to central Newfoundland to handle the labour unrest. On a picket line at Badger, Constable William Moss of the Newfoundland Constabulary was injured. He died two days later. To end the labour strife, Premier Smallwood outlawed the IWA and set up another union for the loggers.

HUBERT WATERMAN

TWILLINGATE FISHERMAN

At the time of this story, 1998, Hubert Waterman's family-owned boat was out to the ice, hunting seals. The *Nancy Joanne* had a crew of 10 people. Four were his sons and four were grandsons. A man of the sea, his ear was tuned to the ship-to-shore radio as he told of his life. He started fishing when he was a boy.

I WAS PRETTY YOUNG, and I enjoyed it. I was only about 12 years old when I went with my grandfather and father. We always had motorboats, that was one good thing. Some of the crowd around here never had motors. They had to row.

That first summer, Grandfather, Father, and I fished on the grounds out here.

We fished on the Gull Island Ground, and on good days we would go out on Old Harry, down off Long Point. Then there's another spot below that, Phillip's Spot. Just outside that was Daley's Spot. Below that was Easter Ground and then Young Harry, and then it was Gull Island.

In the fall of the year, I fished the ground out there, too. There's Smoker, Hooper's Ledge, Bread Box, and Fudge's Ground. I know the marks of all the grounds and I know just where to shoot a trawl. We'd go trawling late in the fall, and we'd take up a lot of cod years ago.

That's right out here, sir. I can go out there and take you right on the mark, to put your line right down.

My grandfather and father had schooners. They used to travel to

Labrador years ago. They gave up the Labrador and started fishing off here, handlining and with traps.

I used to cut my tails then, and made a few dollars. Well, if I made $20, that was a lot of money years ago.

My great-grandfather William Waterman died about 84 years ago, when I was a baby. He came out from England and settled down here. He was a tough old gad.

I heard a lot about him. He always ran schooners. In the fall he would go in the bay, woodcutting, for the winter supply of wood. An old guy down here told me they would leave Monday morning, and Saturday night the schooner had to be out of the bay again, with a load. He didn't allow any slack.

My grandfather was born here, Skipper John Waterman. He ran into island ice [an iceberg] going to Labrador, and sank his schooner. The iceberg was in the fog and he ran right into her, and beat the schooner up. You know, you never hear talk of them losing any men years ago.

My father, Joseph Waterman, was born right here and built his first motorboat down here. He had a three Hubbard engine in her. That's after they gave up the Labrador. I fished in that old boat, and one Bonfire Night, she drove off her collar. The shackle gave out and she drove in and she beat up.

That fall we went in the bay cutting timber. My brother and I used a pit saw to cut all the timber for father, and he built a boat down in the stage there. We fished in her one year, but the next year Father died of pneumonia.

From that time on, I was on my own. That was when the Depression started, that first year. I was about 18 or 19. I went to the Labrador then, for three years. In Ashbourne's schooner.

I gave that up. I didn't like being a shareman, so I went on my own here in Twillingate.

RICHARD WESTCOTT

THE DOG HARP SEAL

When I interviewed Richard Westcott of Petty Harbour, he was 100 years old. A man with an alert mind and a wealth of memories. Any person who lives for 100 years has seen a lot to talk about. Here is the story about the time he crossed the path of a dog harp seal out at the seal fishery.

I DON'T KNOW WHETHER it was the year I was in the *Thetis* or no. It must have been the year I was in either the *Thetis* or the *Diana*, because there was a man Weir from Petty Harbour, and I was with him that same year.

When you are out on the ice, you get separated, quite a distance away from the others. I was walking along the ice that day, by myself. The other man with me was far enough away that I couldn't see him.

There was no danger of falling in the water, of being drowned that day, except for walking down into a seal's bobbing hole. They were always there, where the old seal was getting up and down.

It's the harp I'm telling you about. The male harp seal. We always called him the dog harp, and there's a mark on his back. He's all white, but there's a mark on his back. They call it a saddle. The shape of a saddle.

THE DOG SEAL

SO I WAS WALKING ALONG and I looked and I saw this dog. I said to myself I think I'll try to kill him. I didn't have any sense. So I walked over towards him and made a smack at him with the gaff!

He made for me, right savage! And if I didn't back away from him, he'd have eaten me.

He was savage, snarling. But just as I backed up, I could see one bobbing hole, about the size of a barrel, and I kept clear of it. But there was another one there that I didn't see. It was covered over with snow.

I backed right down into it, the same one he was going for. As it happened, I only put one leg down. And I pulled it up just as quick as the dog went down, and he never bothered me.

Whatever way I went into it, I was at liberty to haul my leg up just as quick. Only for that . . .

When I came aboard, I said to Jimmy Weir, "I don't know whether I'd have been eaten or no, but I got one leg down into the dog harp's bobbing hole, after I was trying to kill him. But I got my leg out of the way just in time, and the seal went down."

Jimmy Weir said, "You were some lucky. Do you know there was a man who got his two legs stuck down in the bobbing hole and he couldn't get out of it? The seal went to jump down the hole and squat him to death."

Because there wasn't enough room for the two of them in the one hole.

The dog harp seal is 300 or 400 pounds. He's terrible big, the dog. Now, the female is only about three quarters as big as he is. But it wasn't a female, I guarantee you that.

I never went near one after.

IN THE OLDEN TIMES, like I told you, when the ship would come in from the sealing voyage there would be a fine lot of work at Bowrings and Jobs. That employed a fine lot of men. My father was one of the men who was in the longshoremen's union.

I never heard tell of him seeing anything on the old Petty Harbour Road. They used to walk home on Saturday nights. The next evening, on Sunday, they would bring a stock of grub back out with them. That was partly the reason why they'd come home every Saturday.

There was this man. I was great friends with him and his son. I used to be in his house quite often. He was one of the men who used to work at the same place where my father worked. Two of them were great friends, so we used to visit one another's houses.

I didn't think that he ever saw anything in the ghost story line, but he told me one time, "Richard, I got a terrible fright one night when I was walking home out over the Petty Harbour Road."

"You did?" I said.

"You can say that I did," he said. "I might as well tell you about it. I always used to walk home with a bunch of men."

For some reason or another they were ready to go home and he wasn't. Job's wharf, or Bowrings, was I suppose about half a mile down. They told him they'd wait for him up by the long bridge, farther in town. When he got up there, they weren't there. They were gone ahead.

He knew then he had to walk home without them, the old way, the old Petty Harbour way. That was only nine miles and Goulds way was 12.

So he said he started off, and he went in to Kelly's. Kelly's had a public house up in the west end, up by the crossroads on what they called the Waterford Bridge Road.

When he got on the Kilbride Road he took off and went up over Kenna's Hill. He was coming along, whistling, and didn't have a care in the world until he came around the turn to Long Pond. Around the turn there was a well there.

They called it the Little Well. It was fit to drink out of. So he was going to get a drink out of it, he said, but before he got a chance, here a thing stood right across the road, higher on the legs than any horse he ever saw. And it had this big eye, he said, as big as a saucer, staring right straight at him.

He thought it terrible to turn around and go back. He made a step towards it, and as he did that thing twisted out of his way.

This man had a crippled foot. He used to walk sideways. He forgot he was crippled, he said, and then he started to run. He never stopped running, he said, until he saw the graveyard on the other side of Petty Harbour, up on the hill.

He said he used to trip in stones that were handy as big as footballs. He was so frightened that he couldn't stop running.

When he got over as far as the graveyard, that's where he turned down. He saw the Petty Harbour lights. He was after buying one or two oranges. He took out the oranges and he ate one. That gave him strength to get home to his house. He said he didn't have far to walk to get over, because he lived down in the middle of the harbour. When he got in and opened the door, he fell in across the floor. His father was alive then and he said, "What's wrong?"

"Father, I saw something that gave me a terrible fright."

The next morning was the last day of work in St. John's. They didn't have to go out anymore. And he never got out of bed for two months. He got better, he said, in time to go fishing.

It looked something like an animal, he said. It resembled a horse. He did get some fright.

ART WICKS

FAREWELL EYES!

Art Wicks is one of the best-known fishermen in Newfoundland. He is often heard on radio open line shows talking about the fishery. Here is one of his memories of living in Port Nelson, Bonavista Bay.

THIS IS A REALLY TRUE STORY. Now, up in the other bottom, in the other little cove, the first man to inhabit that was a man by the name of Uncle George White.

Uncle George White came over from Greenspond, and at that time he used to sell wine in jars. It was really common in those days.

Then the law said that you had to go two miles inland before you could sell any wine. So, Uncle George White had to go two miles inland, to a place called John White's Mesh. That's where he built this wine factory. People who came over from Greenspond or anywhere, they had to walk in there, two miles in the country.

Anyway, Uncle George was a real wine drinker himself. At that time, I think our doctor was Dr. Jamieson, one of the early doctors. Uncle George went over and the doctor found something wrong with him.

His eyes weren't all that good and the doctor told him, "You're drinking too much wine. If you drink any more wine you'll go blind."

Uncle George didn't give a damn. If he didn't say goodbye to his drinking, he would lose his eyesight. What was more important?

He turned to the doctor and said, "Farewell eyes!"

A REAL GOOD FRIEND OF MINE, Martin Meadus, told me this. Not only Martin described this, but his wife, Mary King.

He bought a house in St. John's and swore by his Almighty God that this happened. Everybody was gone to bed. About 2:00 he heard somebody down putting the kettle on the stove. Then someone went and flushed the toilet. By and by, the lights all went out.

It wasn't long before it got to him. This night he couldn't put up with it any more. Someone was rattling the forks.

Mary said one time she was going down over the stairs and she met this old fella coming up. She didn't know who he was. Mary sat in the corner right there when she told me that. It is enough to frighten the lights right out of you.

This is as true as God in Heaven. Martin was sitting down there, sir, when he told me.

This night he got up in the bed and this presence came in the room. He said, "You could hear the drawing of breath."

Martin said, "For the love of God, give me some peace. Take whatever you want."

They never heard of him after.

Mary told me, "Art, my dear, the chandeliers were shaking."

Martin and Mary got rid of the house. They are sure that house is haunted.

I said, "Mary, is that true?"

"That's true, Art."

YEARS AGO IT WAS NOTHING UNUSUAL for someone in the community to be seeing a ghost. It was almost a routine thing to be seeing some kind of a light or some kind of a schooner coming in the harbour with full-rigged sails. And boy, it really did happen.

I can recall one night coming home from Shambler's Cove. It was years ago. I was in a rowboat. I would say it happened about 1:00 in the morning when this red light came in from the eastward. It came in but it didn't make any noise and was just about to hit the boat. It frightened the living daylights right out of me. I didn't know what it was. I thought it was someone in a boat, a speedboat or some damn thing, but it didn't make a noise. It just disappeared. That was off, backward off Burry's Point, this red light.

There was another time in Greenspond Tickle. We call it Greenspond now. We always made fun at people telling us that there was a light. But this night, a big red light, about the size of a puncheon, came on down through the tickle. It frightened the living daylights out of everyone. It just went on down through and disappeared. So I don't know, really, if it was a ghost light or what the devil it was.

I was talking to Captain Sam Blackwood. He always had the schooner called the *Maggie Blackwood*. Sam was courting a girl in Port Nelson, Flossie White.

He told me scores of times about a place called Coaker's Rocks, two big rocks over in Safe Harbour. He said going up, especially in a haze or a dense fog or a little bit of snow, he could see this light coming out from the woods. Before the light got out to where Sam was, it always disappeared.

THE FIRST WICKS

THIS OLD FELLA WICKS, he moved to Port Nelson first. When he came in he built a house right by the seashore, I would say no more than 15 feet from the shore, a kind of a two-storey house.

At that time the place was densely populated with wood. There were birch trees up in our garden, a good two, three hundred birch trees, and some were as big around as a barrel.

The old fella Wicks went to cultivate some land there and he came across this coffin. No one seems to know why it was there. They think it was from a pirate ship that came in long before that.

Now, the man who took the coffin up, that was Alfred Wicks. He took up the coffin to make an ice-hunting box from it. Grandfather told me the board was just as dry as could be. In those years, people carried an ice-hunting box to the seal fishery. It was a real heavy, crude box.

Whoever the man in the coffin was, he was a tall guy. He had blond hair, but when he opened the box he just disintegrated. They don't know who it was, a Norwegian, or a pirate, or someone else.

He didn't live there. He had to be brought in on some ship

steamer or schooner. He probably had died or someone killed him aboard a boat.

Perhaps they dug him up because they thought there might be some money.

Most generally pirates would have some money, but there was none there. The only thing he found was the body.

Years ago I think I was carried aboard the boat wrapped up in Uncle Jim Wicks's oil jacket. The first boat he had, he brought her home from Quirpon. He was down there with my father. My father fished with him, and Grandfather, on the grounds.

When I got old enough, I had to go. We had no choice because everybody in the family at that time, which was eight or nine of us, we all helped with the chores, with the fish, and in the gardens.

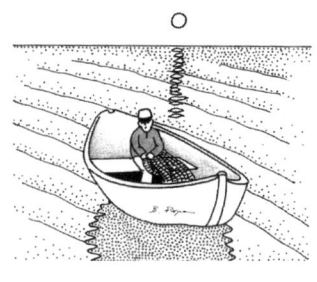

We were taken out of school at a very early age. If the father thought he had to take you out of school, he did. He figured what's the use of education anyway? They carried you out in the fishing boat, and then in the winter they took you back in the woods.

I can recall going out in boat and being seasick as a dog, praying to God that there'd never be another fish caught in them days. But as time progressed, I got away from thinking like that, and this became my way of living.

You had to get out there in your own boat and do your own thing. We most generally fished the inshore grounds. Flowers Island grounds.

At that time there were fluctuations in the fishery during them years. Some years you did good, some years you didn't do nearly as good. In those days, all the fish caught was salted and dried.

Handlining, that was the main thing. They handlined and they used the dapper with caplin for bait. Father didn't use a trap. He used cod nets and a trawl.

We would fish anywhere from three to four miles from Port Nelson, out on the Flowers Island ground. There were all kinds of places there. There were Three Rock Shoal ground, Ireland, and Jimmy Green's Knob, and I could go on and on. Everybody went on the fishing grounds in them years by knowing fishing marks. We could use a house in Wesleyville or a house in Safe Harbour or a church there to position ourselves. The church was a really good landmark for people to get on the ground.

The Labrador Gull

I'LL TELL ANOTHER STORY ABOUT GRANDFATHER, who used to fish with Skipper John Blackwood in a schooner called *Tulip*. Grandfather said to me, "Now, you look out to the pigs when I'm gone to the Labrador and I'll bring you home a gull."

Now that was something. Everybody wanted a gull as a pet. They were captured on the Labrador, put in a crate or something, and brought home.

In the fall, Grandfather came home on the schooner. Skipper John Blackwood threw the crate up on the wharf. "Here's your gull now, Art. Look out for him."

Before he went in the house, Grandfather said, "I think I'll go up now and see how the pigs are."

He went up and looked at the pigs. When he saw the shape they were in, he came down on the wharf. He turned to Pete Blackwood or someone. "Come here, Pete. I want you. Here's a gull for you."

Pete grabbed it. "What's the reason you never gave the gull to Artie?"

Grandfather said, "I don't think he looked out to them pigs very well while I was gone. The pigs are that poor, you have to tie a knot in their tails so they won't go through the fence!"

Our Winter Playground

I CAN SEE IT NOW. The harbour frozen over. The ones who owned the schooner frozen in the ice lived in Greenspond. They wouldn't know about us going aboard.

We would sneak aboard and go down in the cabin. We also would light a big fire in the forecastle.

A buddy of mine, Victor Burton or someone else, would get some potatoes. He got the potatoes, and someone else got the carrot, and we would go aboard the schooner. Someone would swipe a bit of salt meat out of the barrel, not very much. We went aboard the schooner, put the funnels up, and put on the biggest kind of a scoff.

I recall one night. I'll tell the story. It's not all true, but there was something to it. The part about the overalls is not true.

Victor Burton said, "Now Art, we're going aboard the schooner tonight to cook up a scoff. I'll get the turnip, carrot, and all that."

There were half a dozen of us together. He said, "What are you going to get for mutton, you know, fresh meat?"

"Boy," I said, "I don't know."

Now, in December the old people would kill a sheep and they would hoist it up into a gambol. A gambol is a frame of sticks between its legs, and that's how they would wash and clean it. It wouldn't take long for that sheep to freeze in those years, only overnight.

So I said, "It's no trouble to get mutton. Me and Grandfather killed a sheep this evening."

I went down in the night, about half past seven or 8:00, when everything was quiet, December month. I chopped the mutton off, there is no doubt about that.

Now Grandfather had a dog, Rover her name was. He thought the world of that dog. Rover heard everything, every little crack. Grandfather knew if there was someone around, by Rover barking.

So this night, no mistake, I was down in the store. I had this big five-cell flashlight, the only thing we had then. We found the axe on the bench and I said to Vic, "You hold on the flashlight and train it on the mutton hanging down."

Just as I was going to make the chop at some meat, the flashlight went out. Instead of chopping the meat, I chopped off the rope.

At that time I was wearing a big pair of overalls two sizes too big for me. Instead of the mutton coming down and falling down on the floor, it went down inside of my overalls. Here I was now, with the two hooves down in the overalls, and here was the dog barking!

I could hear Grandfather out there shouting, "There's something down in that store!"

The next morning he said to me, "What was Rover barking about last night?

"I don't know," I said.

"I should have gone down last night."

He went down in the morning and found part of the mutton on the floor. "Art," he said, "are you sure you don't know who was there?"

Now, Grandfather thought the world of me. I could do nothing wrong. Even if I told him I did it, he would say, "No, that was someone else did that."

He would blame it on Eric Blackwood or some of the boys. "Cocky, my son, if you finds him who did that, let me know!"

"Yes, I'll sure let you know, Grandfather."

THAT DAY IS GONE

WAY BACK IN THEM DAYS, everybody respected each other. You wouldn't dare go and take someone else's berth. We respected others' property. And everybody helped one another. If I wanted to pull up my boat, everybody was there with a willing hand.

I hate to say this. You could go up on the wharf today and you bring up a conversation about someone. "You know, he's got a crab licence." Or say, "Someone else haven't got a crab licence."

He could push you over the wharf! I'll tell you, that's how heated the debate has gotten these days. Because if one segment of the fishery closes, down people think they had to get in on the new fishery too.

There is a lot of animosity, and boy, there's a lot of greed over the quotas.

But it wasn't like that years ago, not in my recollection. If you didn't have a bit of paint, someone would bring a bit of paint to you. They would tell you where a little bit of fish was to be found, but today it's altogether different.

Now, you could go out here on the slip and you could scote the living daylights out of you. They wouldn't even lift a hand or turn an eye towards you. But years ago people would be glad to help. Every opportunity, they helped you pull up your boat.

There was one thing that really amazed me. Every year before the schooners went to the Labrador, they would come in by the wharves and would heave down. However, many men were in that community, 50 or 60, and sometimes women, would go and give that skipper a helping hand to heave down his boat. The boat was tipped on its side so the bottom could be cleaned and caulked and painted.

There were a lot of houses belonging to older people that died. They were on the other side of Port Nelson, about 300 or 400 feet across the tickle, probably half a mile. If a man had bought a house there, he would wait until the harbour was frozen over solidly. He would go rig the house out. Then he put a flag up when he was going to move.

Boy, you'd better believe the people would be going in droves. People were only too glad to go and help others.

Everyone was community-minded. Everybody had a helping hand for someone else. I hate to say it, but that day is gone.

THE SHAG ROCK ACCIDENT

I'M NAMED AFTER MY UNCLE Art Wicks. He and my father and Jim Wicks had a hunting accident.

In the winter of 1917, in January, they left Port Nelson in a rowboat to go duck hunting down on what we called Shag Rock, off Greenspond.

They left around 4:00 in the morning, cold enough to perish you in them years, and vapour flying. My Uncle Art Wicks and Jim landed on Shag Rock. They went up over the island there in order to shoot ducks as they flew in. My father stayed aboard the boat until he heard the gun. That was an indication that they had killed some ducks, and he would row out around to get them.

He heard the gun and he rowed out around. He didn't see anything, so he wondered what happened. He landed the boat and walked up over, only to find, to his amazement, that Jim had shot Father's brother, Uncle Art.

They were crawling along, and I supposed he must have hit the cap on the muzzle-loader. Father was only 17 or 18 years old, I think. Well, you can imagine the panic that he was in, and Jim as well.

Jim was a big man, 200 pounds, I suppose. He had the job of getting Uncle Art down aboard the boat and lash him down in the boat and tie him to the risings. He had to row in then.

They went in and landed at Uncle Ned Blackwood's place, and that's where they kept them until they got settled down. Then four or five men went out and brought in my uncle.

That was a very sad story. That really happened.

RESETTLEMENT

WHEN A MAN GROWS UP in a place, his roots are there. "You can take a man from the bay but you can't take the bay from a man," the saying goes.

So when you live there and you build up a fishing premises, your roots are there. It's some hard to tear up stakes and go somewhere that you don't know, into a welfare state.

While they were there in the outports, they were independent. They could fish and they could do all kinds of things, but government encouraged them to move to some kind of inland town. This is what happened when centralization came in, resettlement.

At that time the government was under Joey Smallwood's regime. He paid so much to move a house. One hundred dollars, 200 dollars. It wasn't very much, but people I suppose grasped that opportunity. Because money then was something that was very scarce, so people did get a little bit for moving.

As one family left, it made it harder for the other people to survive, to keep the whole society going. Then they got down to the point where the teacher left. You know what that meant. When the school goes, there goes rural communities.

Anyway, I was the last one to pull up stakes. They had all gone and I was the last family. Apart from Uncle Baxter Whiteway, an old man who lived on the other side of the cove, by himself.

But I was the last family. I was married. I had three kids. They had a bit of schooling, so what could I do? I had no other choice. I decided I would move over here to Badger's Quay. I didn't know what the future held for me after I left there, no more than the man in the moon.

I was the fella they hired to rig out the houses for moving. I rigged almost every house over at Safe Harbour and brought them over here. The houses that are down here now in Safe Harbour Square, I was the guy who went over there and put runners in under them, put casks into them, and floated them over here and brought them up here to where they are standing now.

I'm the man, Art Wicks.

After a few different jobs, I got a boat and I got an engine. I went lobster fishing then, I guarantee you. I'm not blowing my own horn, but if I didn't get lobsters or fish, I'd want to know the reason why.

I was out there when the weather wasn't fit. I shouldn't be saying this, but I've seen some longliners come back, afraid of the weather, but I would go out. Everybody said to me, "You're crazy."

I don't know, probably I was, but I had a lot of experience on the water when I was growing up young. I guarantee you, I was never found in here with my legs dangling over the wharf. I wasn't a hangashore, afraid of the water.

I recall the union had a strike on here. They were talking about the scarcity of fish.

Bill Short came down here with the union. I was a regional representative. We were living in the old house then, and I was down on the wharf. I was doing trawl lines, putting on sud lines, getting ready to go trawling. He said, "Art, I'll help you."

I said, "No problem. You can help me put on a few sud lines."

We ran out of sud lines and Bill said, "You got some more?"

"Yes. They're there in that store."

He went to the store on the wharf. The next thing I heard was Bill Short swearing.

He came in and threw down the twine. "Art," he said, "I know where you're coming from. I heard you say on the Fisheries Broadcast, 'The Good Lord helps those who helps themselves.' You got 150 quintals of fish there in your store. Where did you get it?"

I said, "I got it while the longliner was tied up to the damn wharf because of bad weather."

So I did. I fished every opportunity I got.

STRANGE THINGS HAPPENED

MY FATHER-IN-LAW was Uncle Skipper Bill Atwood. He owned a schooner. He built her, rigged her out, and sailed her to Labrador. The name of the schooner was the *Parallel*. Now that's a queer name, isn't it? He built the schooner and he called her the *Parallel*. Often people wondered why he would would ever call the schooner the *Parallel*.

Anyway, he had a fella aboard, Peter Feltham. He was a hard case.

There was a place over here on Pool's Island what they called Paddy Poor, a little island, and they said this fella was drowned, Paddy, but they don't know who in the devil he was. Paddy Poor.

There was a light, the token of this fella, always coming down through the tickle. Someone remarked, "There's Paddy Poor coming."

And old Peter Feltham said, "Come aboard, you old so-and-so."

My mother said the light came and rested on top of the schooner. It shook the living daylights out of the schooner, the sails, the whole lot.

You can believe that or not. My mother told me that, and she didn't tell any lies.

Uncle Isaac Wakely was the first man to live over in a place called Candle Cove, a little place no bigger than this kitchen, and right in the centre of the cove on that side there's a rock shaped like a candle.

Near that was Isaac's Droke. Poor Sam Blackwood, he used to go up to Port Nelson to see Flossie White. He told me, "Art, boy, it's an awful queer thing. Nights we have gone up there and saw the smoke coming out from Isaac's Droke."

I said, "Sam, did it scare you?"

"No boy, that's something else. If someone told me about it, I might get scared, but seeing this stuff in person, it wasn't scary." I believe that too.

There's another story. We lived in Port Nelson, this little place, and we had a schoolhouse down there, right in the bottom. Old Skipper Leez Blackwood's funeral was held in the schoolhouse.

Uncle Jim told me, my father told me, and my grandfather told me that they would go up in the mornings to go in the woods. They had to pass behind the schoolhouse and go in the woods or to get a turn of water. When Uncle Jim would go up, there would be a woman with no head, standing on the bridge.

When the school was sold, Father bought the school, and you know what? As true as God the devil made . . . and he built a store out of it. I mean, geez, old man, we were frightened to death. He took the lumber out of the school to build it, and there were times that I didn't go out in that store, frightened to death.

I'm telling you a true story.

Now then, I'm going to tell you another story. This man who I'm referring to, he was a Christian man. He was a lay reader in the church. That was Uncle Elias Burry.

The night that the *Ella M. Rudolph* was lost, he was lying down. The man told me that himself, a Christian man, lying down on that couch. He told me time and time again, that night the door came open and in came Poor Sam Carter, oilclothes and all on, with a lantern in his hand. He stood right in the middle of the room with water dripping down.

Sam Carter was lost that very night on the *Ella M. Rudolph*. By geez, that was able to make you shiver. Elias Burry told me that time and time again.

ABSALOM "UNCLE APS" WILLIAMS

THE DIRTY LYNX

Uncle Aps Williams was born in Porcupine Bay, Labrador. He spent all his life fishing and fur trapping. He was living in Cartwright when he told this story. Since then he has moved to Goose Bay.

I NEVER GOT IN ANY TROUBLE with very many wild animals, clear of a lynx one time. Natives claim he's a mountain cat. But lynx is the right name.

You would get so anxious to get back to your stopping place. Well, you had to get wood for the night and all kinds of stuff like that. Perhaps you were hungry, after all day with nothing to eat.

You might take something in your game bag to eat, perhaps, but it was so miserable cold. It was all frozen up, anyhow. If you had food it was all frozen too hard, and it was hardly any use to start a fire outdoors. You wouldn't have time to thaw that up in the fire. You'd only burn it up. So you waited until you got back, in the night. But you had to be careful not to rush too much, or you could get in trouble.

They get around in families, the lynx. If they had a brood one year, the young stayed on to the next year. They might have 10 or 12 into a family. I caught one of them little fellas over across the river on the other side. I was just about a mile from home camp.

It was getting dark. The sun was gone down. When I got over there to the bank, I got up over it, and here was a lynx peeking out around a stick at me, and another one in that trap. A big one, too.

The old one in the trap was lying down. I scravelled up and took it out, a great big old cat. In a hurry, I just slung it alongside. I hooked out the trap, and tailed it again. I got the bedding put over it.

I slewed around, and I grabbed my cat by the back of the neck. I was going to pick him up. I thought he was dead. But he started drawing right up! My gosh, I didn't know what to make of it. I put both my hands onto him, and grabbed him hold, but his old legs were so long, and the old claws so merciless. They were kicking but they were away from me.

I didn't know what to do. The gun was there up against the tree. At last I hove him down and jumped on him with both feet. I had one foot on his neck and one on his back, behind his shoulders.

It was something to keep up, and he was nearly beating me. He was nearly getting out from under me, but I grabbed my gun. It was only a single shot .22 and you know it was a hard job to get the bullet to go in the chamber.

So I thought about it. I took my gun and I started tapping him on the head, but I was afraid to hit too hard. I thought I'd break my gunstock. But I gave him quite a whack, though, and kind of dazed him a little bit. But you know, their heads are some hard. The lynx's skull is some hard.

So I got a cartridge in, and I put the muzzle of the gun to his head. But you know what happened? Their heads are kind of flat and the bullet went up over. It never went in! It just bounced up over. That's the only time that I ever thought I was in trouble.

I had a guy with me one time. I used to be trapping with him a lot. He was a Williams fella, a cousin of mine. He told me he did the very same thing one time by himself.

He caught a cat that he thought was dead. He had his snowshoes on. When he discovered he was alive, he hove him down and jumped on him with the snowshoes. His gun was hung up and it was hard to load, trying to keep the cat from getting away. The snow was quite soft and the lynx kept working his way out. Just like my lynx.

I'll never forget that one. That was about the only dirty one ever I had.

WHEN I WAS 17, I had a strange thing happen to me. I boxed a gun. I was baiting a trap for a fox when this bird came along. I wanted him, so I fired at him. I don't know why my gun busted.

The powder and a piece of metal stuck in my forehead. I went down on my hands and knees. I don't know how long I was there, face and eyes down on the rocks. I was smerting and I couldn't open my eyes.

You know what black powder is—terrible stuff to smert and cut. It's like lye. I was some bad for a long time. I was lucky, because if the piece went in there proper, it would have killed me.

I wasn't very far in. Only about 12 miles. I never got back to my cabin until it was after dark. Every now and then I'd have to get down on my hands and try to rest. I was frightened and I never had anything to wipe myself.

When I came to a bit of water, I washed my eyes. That would make it a little better. I would wash out the blood that was running in my eyes and this old black powder mixed with it, cutting, cutting.

That was in the fall. Home, we were isolated. We wouldn't see doctors or nurses until the run froze up. Then the nurses or a doctor would come around on a trip by dog team.

A nurse come down, an English girl, oldish too.

She said, "I tell you what's going to happen to you. That powder is just like lye. Tell the doctors to give you an X-ray on your head and have them skin it off and scrape the bone, because that could go in through the bone. There's a little thin vellum over your brain, and if it goes through that it would give you a bad time. You could go in a coma and never know anything."

It nearly happened to me.

After years, it was just like the head was coming off me. But I never had that done. I should have done it. I don't feel it. As I got older, it wore away from me.

JAMES S. YOUNG

SHIPWRECKED ON THE SS *BRUCE*

Sidney Bond Young left Twillingate Island to go to the mainland for work. The year was 1911. His son, James S. Young of Twillingate, tells the story of his father's trip aboard the SS *Bruce*, a passenger ferry on the Gulf.

FATHER WAS BORN IN 1894. He always got very seasick. He'd throw up until he couldn't stand up in the boat. That was the reason, at 17, he left and went up to Toronto.

He had a half-brother, a construction foreman, living up in Toronto, and that's where he aimed to go. Father worked at that until he got enough money to change jobs and get in with the police.

He went with the Ontario Metro Police and remained with them for 10 years, during which time he rose to the rank of Sergeant. At the time he was stationed in Windsor, and it was here he accepted a position with General Motors as an assistant plant engineer. He remained with GM for the next 31 years, until retirement in 1958.

Father was gone for years before he returned. He was 17 when he left and he didn't come back until Come Home Year, 1966. He died at age 95.

AN ACCOUNT FROM SIDNEY YOUNG, TWILLINGATE

I WAS BORN IN TWILLINGATE, Newfoundland. I left Twillingate for Toronto on March 17, 1911, aged 17, with my parents' blessing. My half-brother, Louis Gillett, who lived in Toronto for seven years, begged my parents to let me come to Toronto.

We had to go by motorboat from Twillingate to Lewisporte, then by train to Port aux Basques. We left there at 11:30 p.m. on a steamer, SS *Bruce*, March 23, to cross the Gulf of St. Lawrence for North Sydney.

About 4:30 a.m., March 24, the steamer ran aground on the Scateri Island, Louisbourg, Nova Scotia, 18 miles from where we were supposed to go.

There was a high sea rolling and we had been going through broken ice all night. When the steamer hit the solid rock, all the lights went out and the passengers were thrown out of their beds. The steamer fell over on its side, exposed to the gulf.

This allowed every sea to go over her. The steamer had four lifeboats. Two of these were smashed to pieces and two passengers were drowned in front of me.

The captain gave orders that women and children were to be taken off first. Due to the high sea, the other two lifeboats had to row four miles to land the passengers, and get word to the mainland for them to send a rescue boat.

Due to the fact that it took so long for a boat to row eight miles, four each way, a rescue steamer arrived before all the passengers had been taken off.

It was 4:00 p.m. when the steamer from Louisbourg came to take the rest of us off.

We were given dry clothing and lots to eat, then taken to North Sydney, where I took the train for Toronto. I arrived in Toronto March 25, 1911.

MILLIE YOUNG

PORT AU PORT MIDWIFE

Millie Young learned the skills of a midwife the old way. She learned by going with another midwife on her visits to pregnant women. Mrs. Young had a full, busy life, raising a large family. At the same time, she helped to deliver hundreds of babies in western Newfoundland.

THEY DID CALL ME MILLIE all the time, but my right name is Mildred. Victor T. Young and Rose Anne Felix were my parents. I was born out in Lourdes. They used to call it Clam Bank Cove before it got named Lourdes.

I helped deliver 550 babies. In Lourdes, Three Rock Cove. Black Duck Brook. Winterhouse and down to Cape St. George.

First I went around with Mrs. Henry Skinner. She was a very good midwife. Every time there was a baby born, I'd always be with her, so I learned from that. Then I went around with a doctor.

I started when I was in my early thirties. I had 11 children myself. I was pregnant the first trip I went on a maternity case. I even delivered four of my sister's children. The last baby I delivered was in West Bay. In the '50s.

Back then there were no cars. In the summer, when you had to go they used to have a horse and cart, and in the wintertime it was by horse and sleigh. If I was called out on a stormy day, I had to go. I wrapped up in blankets. I went out in bad days, big storms.

After the baby was born, probably, if it was far away, like Three Rock Cove or Black Duck Brook, I always stayed three to five days, until the woman got up. I'd wash the baby and the baby's clothes, and if she had children, wash their clothes and cook meals for them. I'd do all that. For women who lived closer to me, I'd visit every morning.

I had 11 children myself, and I made all their clothes on a sewing machine. I still got the sewing machine in there, an antique Singer. And I used to wash all their clothes. I only had a big galvanized tub, and a washboard.

I baked our bread and pies. I used to make wedding cakes for people.

I was pretty poor off until I started to get my Baby Bonus. I used to do all that work for $10, on a case like that. Ten dollars to work there for five days' work. It came to nothing. I worked hard all my lifetime. I'll never forget it.

The hardest part was getting up all hours of the night. I'd be so tired of working all day, out in the garden. But I loved the job, though.

INDEX

GARRY CRANFORD was born in Markland, Trinity Bay, and grew up in Buchans (Central Newfoundland) and New Harbour (Trinity Bay). He is the owner of Flanker Press, the largest trade book publishing firm in Newfoundland and Labrador, founded in 1994 and based in St. John's. He is also the owner of Pennywell Books, an imprint of Flanker Press that specializes in literary fiction, short stories, drama, essay collections, young adult fiction, and children's books.

A proactive campaigner for the preservation of this province's culture and heritage, Garry Cranford is author, co-author, and editor of many non-fiction books dealing with the history of Newfoundland and Labrador, including *Norma & Gladys*, *The Buchans Miners*, *Potheads & Drumhoops*, *From Cod to Crab*, *Tidal Wave*, *Not Too Long Ago*, *Our Lives*, and *Sea Dogs & Skippers*.

He has two children, Justin and Jerry, and two grandchildren, Nicholas and Grace, and lives in St. John's with his wife, Margo.